Winning the Wealth Game Using Property

How You Can Make Money and Become Wealthy With Property

Mark Robinson and Lars Huttner

Copyright © 2014 by Winning the Wealth Game PTY LTD

ISBN: 978-1-922093-08-0

All rights reserved, including the right of reproduction in whole or in part in any form.

First Edition 2014

No part of this book may be reproduced without written permission from the publisher or copyright holder, except for a reviewer who may quote brief passages in a review; nor may any part of this book be reproduced, stored in a retrieval system, or transmitted in any form or by any means electronic, mechanical, photocopying, recording or other, without written permission from the publisher or copyright holder.

This book is designed to provide accurate and authoritative information in regard to the subject matter covered. It is sold with the understanding that neither the author nor publisher is engaged in rendering legal, accounting, or other professional services by publishing this book. As each individual situation is unique, questions relevant to personal finances and specific to the individual should be addressed to an appropriate professional to ensure that the situation has been evaluated carefully and appropriately. The author and publisher specifically disclaim any liability, loss, or risk that is incurred as a consequence, directly or indirectly, of the use and application of any of the contents of this work.

Limit of Liability/Disclaimer of Warranty

Whilst the publisher and author have used their best efforts in preparing this book, they make no representations or warranties with respect to the accuracy or completeness of the contents of this book and specifically disclaim any implied warranties or merchantability or fitness for a particular purpose. No warranty may be created or extended by sales representatives or written sales material. The advice and strategies contained herein is intended for a general audience and does not purport to be, nor should it be construed as, specific advice tailored to any individual and may not be suitable for your situation.

Examples in these materials are not to be interpreted as a promise or guarantee of earnings. Earning potential is entirely dependent on the efforts and skills of the person applying all or part of the concepts, ideas and strategies contained herein.

Neither the publisher not the author shall be liable for any loss of profit or any other commercial damages, including but not limited to special, incidental, consequential, or other damages.

Best Seller Success Publishing
Sydney, Australia
Las Vegas, Nevada, USA
+1 (702) 997 2229
+61 (02) 8005 7441

Special Offer

Would you like to find out if property is the right vehicle for your situation?

Book in right now for your **FREE** investment property strategy session, your bonus for reading this book.

To Grab Your Bonus Session go to

www.WinningtheWealthGame.com.au/propertybookoffer

In this personalized session you will get a property plan tailored just for you.

We'll discuss what options are available for you and what your next step is.

About Mark Robinson

Mark Robinson, founder and CEO of Acquire Wealth Solutions loves nothing more than helping Business Owners and Property Investors set up, grow and protect their wealth. His actions speak for themselves, creating seven successful companies in a four year period as well as a charity dedicated to a hand-up not a hand-out approach. His last company broke even in three months, profitable in six and hit a six-figure income in nine months. His clients describe Mark as very professional and proactive with his advice.

Mark has written seven books and has been involved with over $365 million dollars worth of property transactions for his clients. Mark has an ability to translate the complexities of the modern financial world into a simple easy-to-understand language.

This allows his clients to grasp his recommendations with the understanding required to succeed. Mark uses a simple formula that looks at where you are today, where you want to be and then we work out which steps will be the best for you to get you there. Mark always works with the end in mind. What you are trying to achieve is foremost in his mind. Mark has the ability to help you take what you have learnt in seminars, webinars etc, and turn it into a viable and actionable financial plan.

This means we can look at all scenarios and not be stuck with traditional thinking. We will look at property, shares, managed funds, superannuation and businesses. You see most traditional Financial Planners will only look at managed funds because they just do not understand property or business. "Why planners overlook property and businesses is beyond me" Mark states.

Mark loves helping business owners increase their profits and exposure using the latest information and technology, such as Infusionsoft, Facebook, Twitter and LinkedIn.

Personal

Mark lives in beautiful Sydney with his wife Billie and two gorgeous girls, Jasmine-Rose and Riley-Jane. He loves nothing more than spending time with his family either relaxing by the pool or down at the park or beach. He loves to travel and has spent time in Europe, Asia, USA, New Zealand and has been across most of Australia.

Education and Experience

Licensed Financial Planner. Diploma in Financial Services and Financial Planning. Diploma in Financial Services Mortgage Broking. Mark Robinson is an Authorized Representative, No 243170 of My Planner, and AFSL No 345905

Mark has authored and co-authored a number of books. The Wealth Game and Winning the Wealth Game book series.

Titles include:

Winning the Wealth Game by Protecting Your Assets

Winning the Wealth Game in Business

Winning the Wealth Game by Creating Multiple Streams of Income

Winning the Wealth Game Using Shares

Winning the Wealth Game Using Property

Winning the Wealth Game Online

Winning the Wealth Game in Network Marketing

Helping Business Owners and Property Investors to set up, grow and protect their Wealth is his mantra

Mark is known as Australia's leading wealth protection and creation expert. After writing *Seven Steps to Wealth Protection* and *Your Path to Wealth*, he has written *Winning the Wealth Game in Business* a step-by-step guide that tells you how you can be successful in business and become wealthy, all in 9 simple steps and has now completed the second book in the series, Winning the Wealth Game Using Property, a guide that shows you how you can make money with property. You won't believe how easy it is with this book!

About Lars Huttner

Lars Huttner is a qualified Financial Planner with 10 years investment experience. Lars caught the investment bug at the age of 27 when he and his wife decided to build their first investment property -- a small 4x2 near where they lived. That property is now worth double what it cost them to build. But subsequent property investments didn't work out so well. Lost jobs and other causes of financial stress, including the death of his father-in-law, a co-investor, undermined the investments. But each investment taught harsh but valuable lessons.

Helping other people avoid those harsh lessons is the basis behind Lars' Financial Planning business. His passion is property and helping people get what they need to make their dreams come true, be it that holiday they have always wanted, the new car, to retire early or to acquire 15 hot properties.

Lars now has several buy and hold properties, developments and different share strategies on the go with a view to grow into other asset classes to diversify further. Lars uses his personal experience of different investment strategies to ensure that what he recommends to his clients is the right fit for them.

Lars continues to expand his knowledge of investment options, regularly attending seminars and workshops as well as throwing his own time and money behind different strategies since he will rarely recommends a strategy he hasn't tried himself. Lars not only thoroughly researches his investment strategies, but encourages his clients to do the same, as he believes that everyone who wants to invest should have at least a basic understanding of the investment choices they are making. And that is one of the reasons why Lars has chosen to co-author this book!

Education and Experience

Licensed Financial Planner. Diploma in Financial Planning. Lars Huttner is an Authorized Representative, No 461452 of My Planner, and AFSL No 345905

Personal

Lars lives in Perth with his wife and three children. He enjoys Pina Coladas and walks in the rain.

A Note From the Author

So why write this book and spill all of these 'top secrets' of the rich & wealthy? I have a vision of the future that I would dearly like to see come true. This vision does not include only myself and my family, my friends and their extended families, it involves as many people as I can get to listen to what Mark and I have to say. These people need to accept the challenge of making their lives extraordinary, setting themselves up to throw off the shackles of working for money and instead having their money work for them, having more financial freedom and most important of all, having more time. Time for family. Time for fun. Time for sleep if they want! Imagine watching your friends go through their morning routine and heading off for their 9 to 5 day while you've woken up and created more wealth while you slept than they will over the next 8 hours? Imagine retiring on more annual passive income than many folks make in their regular day jobs? All these exciting possibilities are within the reach of most of us, all we need is a little push in the right direction and lots of due diligence.

So back to my vision - It has 2 parts. The first part involves raising as many people up to millionaire figures as possible. More millionaires means more spending which strengthens the economy and equals more jobs and a whole pile of flow on effects that benefit our whole country.

The second part is more selfish. It involves a tropical beach, some sort of umbrella drink, lots of sunshine and lots of doing nothing much else. This could be very boring on my own however. You've opened the book so you've taken your first step in the right direction. Join me there? What else is possible?

Lars Huttner

Table of Contents

Winning the Wealth Game Using Property 13
Property Investing – Outlook 21
The Property Market 27
Investing Your Money 33
Types of Property 53
Making Money with Property 59
Capital Growth and Cash Flow 93
Capital Growth vs. Positive Cashflow 105
Buying in Mining Towns 109
Financing 111
Structures 121
Buying in a Self-Managed SUPER Fund 131
How to Make Money from Property During a Recession ... 151
Appendix A: Glossary 153
Appendix B: Property Checklists 169

Winning the Wealth Game Using Property

Property investing is one of the most rewarding wealth creators in Australia – and anyone can be in it. A business owner in particular has both the opportunity and indeed, the need to grow their investment wealth through property investing. A business consumes so much time and money that it is simply good sense to diversify away from having all of one's eggs in the business basket and invest in all kinds of real estate.

Real estate is one of the best industries; it has made more millionaires than any other industry and also has a low barrier to entry for new investors. What's better is that you don't need a degree or any other kind or experience to get into it. All you need is a strong work ethic and desire to learn.

It's my belief that the next couple of years are going to be some of the best for real estate investment. Even though that may be a bold thing to say, let me explain why. A lot of people are still unhappy with the real estate market after the crash, along with the broader economic recession, but that's precisely what makes real estate such a great investment today. Real estate has been on the down for so long, that right now is the time when buyers can take advantage of the best deals.

Of course, I'm not the only person out there who knows this, with big time investors and investment firms already on the move and doing everything they can to get their hands on good real estate opportunities. After all, there must be a good reason why the rich keep on getting richer—they spot opportunities and take advantage of them before it's too late.

Even though most of the population will take about how horrible the real estate market is, these "rich and richer" investors are snapping up real estate like they're hot cakes, preparing to make a new fortune in the process. Don't believe me yet? Well, let's look at some facts:

Supply & Demand:

Remember when you took basic economics back in high school? When supply exceeds demand, prices fall. Well, let's go back in time a few years now before the property market crashed, and you'll notice homebuilders went crazy trying to take advantage of high prices, and overbuilt properties in the process. With an oversupply of housing (this is when supply exceeds demand), prices were naturally going to drop. There are other factors in the real estate crash that made it even worse, but those factors would not have changed the fact that the housing market was going to drop simply because of severe oversupply.

If we fast forward to the mid-crash years, we can see real estate prices dropping significantly while inventory was at an all-time high. No one was able to sell their homes. At this point, homebuilders stopped building new homes—and many were even facing bankruptcy. No one was thinking about starting new projects, with many projects halted mid-way because there was no more funding to complete it.

Now, let's come back to present time. Homebuilders still aren't building (and haven't been for several years), which has caused inventory to shrink. Finally, demand has caught up with supply and homebuyers are finding difficulties in finding a home in some areas—and that trend is spreading throughout the country.

The deeper into economy recovery we go, more and more people are going to be looking to purchase a home (demand is on the rise), however, since no new houses or building have been built, the supply (inventory) is decreasing.

When demand once again exceeds supply, prices will once again rise to what they once were and maybe even higher. This has already started in some areas.

Affordability:

One of the reasons that makes real estate so attractive right now is its affordability. It's cheaper to buy a house in today's market than it is to rent one. Before the crash, property prices were so high that it was far more affordable for most people to rent than buy (in most markets, at least). However, much has changed today. Prices have fallen drastically that has made buying actually more affordable than renting in some parts of the country. When you combine that with increasing levels of confidence that buyers are showing and shrinking unemployment rates, you come up with increased demand.

It's a Unique Time in History

Imagine you were in the market to buy a new vehicle and you found out that a dealership was selling the car you want at 30% less that they paid for it (and you knew that there was nothing with the car. Naturally, you'd think this was a deal not to be wasted. Well it's the same with real estate today—the deals are better than ever; you can buy properties 30% below their value (even more sometimes) because I'm doing it. What does that mean? It means that's a hell of a better deal than the car because the moment you drive that car off, it depreciates by at least 20% -- but right now, properties are appreciating in value. Perhaps not by the levels that we were enjoying pre=market crash, but they're still appreciating.

In today's market I tell investors to not even consider appreciation—that's just a bonus anyway. The true value lies in the fact that these properties can make you very wealthy as rentals. A few years ago, investors would have been over the moon getting a 6-7% cap rate in an investment property—literally, the best rate they could have gotten. Today, however, you can find properties with a cap rate of 10% and more! People aren't as bothered about property appreciating in value when they can make a small fortune through rentals.

Reason Enough?

Now that you understand why property is so hot right now, are you going to be one of the smart investors to take advantage of this once in a lifetime opportunity, or are you going to wait for the next opportunity which may never come?

I knew you'd make the right decision! Now, before you can start building wealth from property, however, you need a plan. A property plan. The section below will talk about the importance of this plan.

The Importance of Having a Plan

Property investment is a business. It's not something you can just walk into blindly and think you'll come out successful, regardless of how easy property is to tap into. Like in any business, you need a plan. In this case, a property plan. The plan should cover everything you need—assess where you are right now, where you want to be in the future and how you're going to get there through property investments.

You can write out a comprehensive business plan if you want, but it's not necessary. A simple business plan does the job fine. Make sure you have specific goals, strategies and deadlines decided upon. To have a specific and more measured plan, ask "who?" "What?" "where?" "Why?" and "how?".

Simply saying I want to make money by investing in property is not a specific enough goals. You need to ask yourself far more specific targeted questions such as:

How will I make money in real estate? I plan to make money by collecting rent ever month. Or, I plan to make money when I sell the investment. How much money do I want to make in the first year? I expect to make a $50,000 profit in the first year.

It's all about making sure you define your objectives and develop specific strategies and plans to meet them. Below are some questions that you should make sure to answer in your plan"

1. What is your goal for investing in property?
2. Do you want to do this as a side job?
3. Do you want to quit your day job and do this full time?
4. Do you want to make a quick profit by flipping a house?
5. Do you want to buy and hold a property for capital appreciation and to make passive income each month?
6. What type of property are you planning on investing in?

   There are almost an infinite number of ways you can invest in real estate, from residential to commercial to industrial. You need to consider all your options and pick the options that meet your goals, finances and personality type. After deciding on the types of property you want to invest in, you want to become an expert in them.

7. How much money will you need to make the initial investment?

   - How will you generate money for the investment if you do not have all of the money on your own?
   - How much do you anticipate monthly expenses will be? Are you realistic with your numbers?
     - Mortgage payment, monthly maintenance, taxes, insurance.

- Are you including a reserve account which will have funds to cover emergency repairs and unforeseen vacancies?
- How much do you anticipate monthly income will be?
- What is the vacancy rate for the area?
- How much can you charge in rent?
- Do you understand how to file taxes for an investment property?

8. How do you plan to market your property?
9. Where will you find tenants?
   - Will you place ads online? In newspapers? On bulletin boards?
   - Do you know how to make your property appealing to prospective tenants?
10. How will you manage the property?
    - Will you be the landlord?
    - Will you hire a property manager?
    - If so, you will need to research management companies or interview superintendents and find out how much they will charge.
11. How will you manage tenants?
    - What will you require upon move-in?

- How much will you charge as a security deposit? Landlords usually charge one to one and a half month's rent.
- How will you select the right tenants?
- Do you understand how to evict a tenant?

12. How will you maintain the property?
    - Will you hire a contractor to perform repairs?
    - Will you do the repairs yourself?
    - Who will take care of yard maintenance (mowing the lawn, shoveling snow)?

13. Do you have a plan if your investment fails?
    - Have you developed an exit strategy? Do you have more than one exit strategy?

Now that you have a basic idea of what is involved and how to move forward, let's move onto the next chapter that outlines some business basics which are essential in the property world.

Property Investing – Outlook

If you've never read Robert Kiyosaki's book, "Rich Dad, Poor Dad", here's what you need to know: In order to get a different result, YOU need to DO something different!

It's time to decide to be wealthy today! Most people don't become wealthy in their lifetimes simply because they don't decide to become wealthy. They (wrongly) assume that getting wealthy is merely for the greedy or the lucky, and they don't have what it takes to become wealthy. The fact is, you don't have to be greedy or lucky to become wealthy, all you need is the determination and conscious decision to take proactive steps that will move you closer towards wealthy.

That's your first big step: making that decision. Announcing to yourself and everyone who can hear that you are going to become wealthy—even if you're currently broke. There's a big difference between being broke and being poor: one is temporary (broke) while the other is a state of mind (poor).

Your next step is to decide what kind of money problems you want to have. You can either be someone who doesn't have enough money, or you can be someone who has too much money. If you want to be wealthy, you need to decide on how you're going to make use of all the extra money you make so you can create even more money. Most people make unnecessary purchases once they get extra money because they haven't decided what to do with the money.

Always think of abundance. Think about having more money that you can make even more money out of. Decide HOW you're going to invest your extra money.

Now that you've decided on the how, it's time to determine exactly where you stand financially and how you're going to move up the financial ladder. Think of your plan as a GPS, even though you know WHERE you want to go, you need to decide on a route (the easiest and most convenient one for you) to get there. And always remember, YOU are in the driver's seat.

Your plan is going to be a step by step guide which will make your journey a lot simpler. After deciding where you want to go and knowing your starting point, you need to plan your journey. Be sure to set up milestones to make your journey less daunting—seeing results along the way is a great motivator.

Your plan should include details on:

1. Getting your money to work for you as much as possible.
2. Getting into the good type of debt that help you make more money. Change your personal debt into investment debt.
3. Investing in excellent real estate that you have researched well and made sure meet your goals.
4. Setting up your finances in a way that helps protect your home and pay off your personal debt do you can focus on investment debt.
5. Ensuring you have a good Plan B (safety net) in cans anything happens. You want to make sure your debts are covered.

6. Reinvesting your profits and rebalancing your portfolio.
7. Reviewing and making adjustments to your plan on a regular basis.

If you're ready to become wealthy and retire early then I can help you. If you're already wealthy and want to become even wealthier, then I can help you too! It all starts with a choice and that choice is yours to make today.

The next piece of advice I'm going to share with you before you embark on your journey isn't about making more money. It's about rewarding yourself. If we worked all the time and didn't make time for fun—time to unwind and relax—we'd grow tired and bored of our journey and may end up giving up on it due to sheer exhaustion. It's very important to take time out and have fun along the way or you'll find the journey a long, boring and possibly difficult one otherwise.

This is why setting up milestones is so important. Every time you reach a milestone, reward yourself. We all deserve some encouragement and pats on our backs, and who better to acknowledge a job well done than yourself? I'm not talking about a lavish reward every time, it could be something that is just significant to you like a weekend getaway for you and your partner...or even just a relaxing night at the movies. What the reward is doesn't matter as much as you actually sticking to the reward plan.

With a plan set in place, your next plan of action is to set a team up to help you. It's important to set up a team you can trust and depend on. Your team must have the mutual goal with you: they will only make money when you make money. This is a great way to motivate them and ensure you have the best team possible looking out for your best interests (as well as theirs).

Get professionals who have more experience than you are, in areas that you're not extremely efficient in. After you have your team and are confident about the people you'll be working with, don't take advice from anyone else. Even though other people might mean well, do that have the professional opinion/experience to back up what they're saying or are they simply giving you their (possibly misguided) opinion?

Think of time as an ally – Patience is your best friend. Any method to make money requires time and patience. Property investment is no different than any other wealth builder, it takes patience and isn't going to happen overnight. The biggest mistake people make is being too impatient, and selling their investments too soon just to see how much profit they made and possibly losing thousands in the process.

Some property investors may not get paid in a few years, which is why patience is so important. Over time, your property can appreciate significantly in value.

Think back to when you bought your house. How much did you pay for it? How much is it worth today? How much will it be worth in ten years? The longer you hold your investments, the more money you can make. This is why it's so important to stay focused on your long-term goals.

Also, be sure to think big. Most people who start small stay small simply because they didn't plan for anything bigger. Your objective is to move out of your comfort zone, stretch yourself to find out how far you can go and really start achieving.

In the words of Jim Rohn, "You don't have to be great to get started, but you DO have to get started to be great." Don't keep holding off and waiting until you think the market is just "perfect" to get started, start TODAY. Start NOW. Move forward by taking the necessary steps to do something different and move towards your journey of financial security.

Set out your goals to replace your income with passive investment income, then once you reach that goal, set a new one to double it. Don't be afraid to be different and doing something that 90% of other, mediocre people aren't doing. By doing something different, you'll also be getting different (better, more rewarding) results.

Your last step is to move forward fast. It's important to act quickly because the right opportunities won't wait for you. You also need to eliminate any excess baggage you may have. If you're hoping to achieve financial success, you need to make a conscious step towards that goal TODAY. It's time to change your mind-set and thoughts.

Read inspirational books or podcasts. Get inspired by listening to what other successful people have been able to achieve and how they did it. Use this information to propel yourself forward and keep a positive state of mind. Because that's what being wealthy is all about in the end. It's a frame of mind. You need to decide to be wealthy and you may even have to remind yourself along the way that you deserve to be wealthy! Define what wealth means to you and pursue it relentlessly until you get it!

The Property Market

The property investment boom

A boom period ended around 2006-07 in most states. That cycle had been going for at least 15 years which had at least five or six years of boom conditions. Right now we are seeing an unwinding of high debt levels rights across the board form private investor-developers to multi-billion dollar property trusts. At the commercial end, business construction will cause an excess of office space, thus pushing back developers' plans. But the cycle is turning and demand will pick up excess stock.

Follow the money

There is a saying in investment markets – "follow the money". This refers to the principle that people and institutions with large amounts of money to invest usually have the means to have conducted a good deal of research before coming to the investment. In property investing one of the cornerstone principles as far as investing in retail housing is to follow the money invested in infrastructure.

Few things create real estate growth more than new infrastructure. This happens because the project improves local services, creates jobs and provides business for local trades people and suppliers, and generates demand for housing.

The great thing about major infrastructure is that it is in the news. You don't need to dig deep to find out where the infrastructure projects; they are almost always news reports issued on major infrastructure projects.

The Basic Principles

No air flight can be undertaken without fuel; similarly the journey towards acquiring real estate requires finance. Of late this 'fuel' for buying property has been much maligned due to the unprecedented global financial crisis which cut a swath through banking and finance companies and Government budgets around the globe. As in any conflagration, truth becomes the victim. Much misinformation has been circulated through the media and intermediaries. Thus, we will guide you, offering you tools and information that will ensure a "full tank of gas!"

Doubtless, the pilot's most important tools are his navigation equipment. Not only for progressing along the designated flight path to the destination but in order to navigate safely through unseen hazards along the way and, importantly, navigation tools that will assist in an assisted landing should weather conditions prevent a visual landing. Winds, turbulence, storms, are all hazards on any flying journey. Property investing, indeed any investing, requires reliable and accurate and timely research. The pilot's instrumentation is 'real time' – nothing else will do.

The penultimate stage of good preparation is the take-off. It's the culmination of the previous stages and ensures that "all systems go". In property investing, the shift of focus is now towards profit and risk management. No journey is without risk and migration strategies are vital for peace of mind. As an investor your goals are to maximise the total returns from an investment and that requires some management of the risks.

Once in cruise mode, there will be less to do. A flight should, well, be 'cruisey". A property investor if they indeed want to maximize their returns needs to consider value-add strategies and ensure that their property is optimally managed for peak performance.

Finally, as the flight begins its descent, preparation for landing commences. In property investing, just as in flying, the time for decent to final exit from the airplane has a degree, its obvious finality. An investment, be it a share or a business or a property needs an exit strategy articulated. Without a clear exit strategy and investment can get buffeted about by head winds and often make poor decisions. Certainly bailing out of a flight mid-air can have rather extreme outcomes!

Is It Safe To Fly Now?

Yes! Airline travel is the safest way to travel, and the safety measures that airlines take to ensure your safety play a big role in that safety track record. Part of the process you're going to learn in this book is how to utilize the same type of safety measures that airlines use to make sure your Real Estate investments are safe and secure also.

The same question needs to be asked of property investing although our premise here is that property is one of the best and safest investments. Your flight takes you to a destination but property is forever.

If you intend to be wealthy; to have a genuine ability to build income outside of your wage or salary then residential property must be the bedrock of your fortune. When you consider any purchase of residential property you may or may not sell it but it will certainly be the cornerstone of building your wealth.

Our program will guide through the steps and strategies necessary to build. Each stage of the journey opens up opportunities to add value, to create income; to generate wealth.

> *"Simplicity is the ultimate sophistication."*
>
> ~ Leonardo da Vinci

One of the great aspects of property investing – at least here in "safe" Australia – is that principles learnt and practices can be applied across different geographic locations and, different types of property and, indeed different decades. Some people may say that the early 1990s were the right time to buy property because land was "cheap" then, compared with the property buyer situation of 2009. The truth is the same principles apply to buying no matter what decade we are living in.

There's a lot of common sense that can be applied to property investing. You need a professional approach to managing and looking after your property. You need to treat your tenants with respect: choose them carefully but respect them as well by not making rents outrageous and keeping the property up to date.

Here in brief we set out the criteria that we believe are the essentials for selecting and buying residential property. These will include the ones mentioned but also criteria such as:

- Price
- Location
- Land content
- Development potential
- Rental yield
- Amenities and many more

These are some the things we believe in; that property investing is above everything else a people business. For sure we need to address the hard-nosed business issues such as research, strategy selection, risk management, documentation, finance but common sense, tried-and-true practices and as throng commitment to win-win outcomes with vendors, buyers, tenants will see you on the path to building wealth.

Investing Your Money

You can do it! It's easier than you think.

No one is born knowing how to save or to invest. Every successful investor starts with the basics—the information in this chapter. A few people may stumble into financial security—a wealthy relative may die, or a business may take off. But for most people, the only way to attain financial security is to save and invest over a long period of time. Time after time, people of even modest means who begin the journey reach financial security and all that it promises: buying a home, educational opportunities for their children, and a comfortable retirement. If they can do it, so can you!

The Two Ways to Make Money

There are basically two ways to make money.

1. You work for money. Someone pays you to work for them or you have your own business.
2. Your money works for you. You take your money and you save or invest it.

Your money can work for you in two ways.

Your money earns money. When your money goes to work, it may earn a steady paycheck. Someone pays you to use your money for a period of time. When you get your money back, you get it back plus "interest." Or, if you buy stock in a company that pays "dividends" to shareholders, the company may pay you a portion of its earnings on a regular basis. Your money can make an "income," just like you. You can make more money when you and your money work.

You buy something with your money that could increase in value. You become an owner of something that you hope increases in value over time. When you need your money back, you sell it, hoping someone else will pay you more for it. For instance, you buy a piece of land thinking it will increase in value as more businesses or people move into your town. You expect to sell the land in five, ten, or twenty years when someone will buy it from you for a lot more money than you paid. And sometimes, your money can do both at the same time—earn a steady paycheck and increase in value.

The Differences Between Saving And Investing

Saving

Your "savings" are usually put into the safest places, or products, that allow you access to your money at any time. Savings products include savings accounts, checking accounts, and certificates of deposit. Some deposits in these products may be insured but there's a tradeoff for security and ready availability. Your money is paid a low wage as it works for you.

After paying off credit cards or other high interest debt, most smart investors put enough money in a savings product to cover an emergency, like sudden unemployment. Some make sure they have up to six months of their income in savings so that they know it will absolutely be there for them when they need it.

But how "safe" is a savings account if you leave all of your money there for a long time, and the interest it earns doesn't keep up with inflation? What if you save a dollar when it can buy a loaf of bread. But years later when you withdraw that dollar plus the interest you earned on it, it can only buy half a loaf? This is why many people put some of their money in savings, but look to investing so they can earn more over long periods of time, say three years or longer.

Investing

When you "invest," you have a greater chance of losing your money than when you "save." The money you invest in securities, mutual funds, and other similar investments typically is not federally insured. You could lose your "principal"—the amount you've invested. But you also have the opportunity to earn more money.

Where should you invest your money and why?

Shares

After the Great Financial Crisis of 2008-09, investors everywhere rightly feel nervous about markets. After all wasn't it the irrational exuberance of investment bankers, inflating their paycheques with worthless securities that sent stock markets and credit markets into a tailspin?

Here's a little secret: the great investors of the world have been quietly buying into markets for months now. They see what's coming and are buying stocks that will double and treble in value of the next few years.

The simple truth is that opportunities abound today. There are companies – indeed countries – that are prospering right now and there are investors in the know who are profiting from the opportunity.

The transformation in share markets over recent decades has been truly amazing. Close to half of all adult people in the UK, in the USA and in Australia, own shares. Why do they do it? Partly because the share market provides one of the best opportunities to achieve your long-term goals.

It's easy, you do not need a lot of money to get started, and shares give you flexibility and control.

When it comes down to connections wisdom, the key to wealth and the answer is quite simple, no, it's not Lotto. Knowledge is the solution. Shares are an important part of any investment strategy and you will find that this book will help you to learn about the stock market and become a successful share investor.

Any investor can buy into a listed company: so you too can enjoy the powerful benefits that stock markets can bring. All you need is a good sense of money management and a sound knowledge of the basics of stock market investing.

First timers

You may never have been an investor; you may think that shares are for wealthy, knowledgeable people. You may believe that shares are the riskiest of all investments. On both counts you would be wrong. Indeed, shares are the safest investment of all asset classes - provided you approach it in a methodical, step-by-step way; learning each step of the way; improving your knowledge, building your skills, learning to manage money and gaining all the time, the skills of an investor.

If you are now ready to make shares an effective part of your investment portfolio you need to answer a few key questions:

- What are my goals?
- How much money should I invest?
- How should I invest?
- What are the tax implications?

Each of these questions is highly particular to each individual but, in general, your age and stage and your capacity to fund a share investment strategy are important. Shares are safe in that you can keep your exposure very, very low while learning – as little as a $100. That may not ever amount to much but it will be a psychological start and it will be the beginning. If you add money progressively, say each month, it may be 12 months or more before you are investing significant amounts. That's' the safety factor.

Understanding the basics

There are a number of types of shares, but the most common and probably the one that you will be most concerned about, at least for the next year or two are "ordinary" shares or "common" stock as they are referred to in the US. These make up the paid up share capital of the company and are listed and traded on the stock market. There are however different types of shares from an investment perspective; here an investor makes choices about whether they are looking for capital growth, for a dividend yield or for a mix.

How do find these? You find these reading about stock markets in the press, in courses, in books and listening to expert commentary.

How to make sense of share prices?

Have you ever been to an auction? Have you ever bargained with a market treader? Why do oil prices fluctuate? It seems perplexing and mysterious; but essentially you need to understand that many factors can simultaneously affect values both positively and negatively over different periods of time. However, the impact of many individual factors is sometimes quite predictable so it can pay to consider them since that is what many other investors will be doing.

Think of the price of a share as being affected by:

- Supply of and demand for the shares
- The inherent value of the shares (a subject for further study)
- Other less direct influences on share prices.

The share market is a market place like any other. The forces of supply and demand determine the price of shares. The more people want to get hold of a particular share, the higher its price will go. If people no longer want a share and few people are willing to buy it, people may have to offer it at a very low price in order to sell it.

The little known technique for staying ahead of the game

Sometimes investors simply are blind to what makes a successful investor. It comes down to one fundamental principle and it's a very easy technique to apply once you are into your strides: *only buy into good businesses.*

The direct impact on a company's share price is the performance of its businesses. Many large businesses like Shell and BHP-Billiton are doing well and continue to please investors (that is not disappoint them with bad news); thus a share price will generally increase in value. It may move around somewhat in the day to day buying and selling and especially move around if boarder economic indicators like a credit crunch impact a market as a whole. Successful companies are businesses that re-invest in their future. They are growing their businesses continuously.

In other words, a share that offers a strong likelihood of capital growth due to reinvesting company profits also has a certain amount of inherent value. The most important factor affecting the price of a share is the company's future earnings prospects, as its earnings will determine the future inherent value of a share. Any changes in forecast earnings, either by company management or by market analysts, will impact the share price.

Past earnings, as can be found in the company's annual report, are an important indicator of a company's earnings ability, but you should also consider the impact of any changes to its business. For example, how will it be affected by a change in senior management, or an acquisition of another business?

Large markets like the New York market which is often reported in terms of a basket of stocks known as the Dow Jones Industrial Average (DJIA) are closely monitored around the world and can impact other markets. This is due to the sheer size of the US stock market as it dwarfs other markets many times over. Again, due to the fact of the US huge economy but also because many investors (large institutional as well as private) hold shares in American companies.

In a similar fashion, although not anywhere near as globally impacting, the UK stock market is often reported on by a broad index of stock known as the FTSE, can impact European markets as London has long been a centre of banking and trade finance for the Continent. It remains one of the world's oldest and largest stock exchanges.

Australia for example, an increasingly India and China, are becoming increasingly significant investment markets. Australians resource companies for example are amongst the largest in the world and many global investors are seeing that India and China have massive populations seeking to expand their economies, see Australian companies as a proxy for these countries.

Four Reasons to Invest in Shares

1. The growth rate of the Australian share market has been an average of 12% per year, according to the Australian Stock Exchange. Though the value of shares fluctuates constantly, marked by occasional bursts and booms, buying quality shares with a long-term view is a solid investment.

2. Shares are easy to buy and sell, which makes them a versatile element of your portfolio.

3. The spread of risk is simple because you can hold shares of multiple companies in several regions.

4. Shares require no physical maintenance or insurance.

Stay tuned for my next book titled "Winning the Wealth Game Using Shares" for more details.

Real Estate

According to APBC research, the most popular investment vehicles in 2007-08 were direct equity, superannuation and residential property. Two thirds of high net worth individuals have residential property investments.

Real estate investments have lost momentum recently in a global setting. Indeed, many HNW portfolios have cut far back on real estate, leaving only about 14% of their overall portfolios in real estate. However, real estate is one of the most stable long-term investments and the real estate market in Australia is particularly attractive right now.

Rental vacancies are at an all-time low in Australia, according to the Real Estate Institute of Australia, which is therefore increasing rent prices. There is a severe shortage of rental properties in Australia's major cities, with Sydney experiencing the tightest shortage with a 0.8% vacancy rate.

Four Reasons to Invest in Real Estate

1. The Australian residential real estate market has grown by 8.5% per year, on average, over the last 50 years, according to the Australian Real Estate Institute. This means that real estate value in Australia have a well-established trend of doubling every 10 years.

2. Though property prices aren't always stable, they are less volatile over the long term than shares are.

3. Buying real estate is a disciplined, long-range investment strategy that nicely complements riskier investments with quicker turnaround times.

4. Property is an investment that most wealthy people are already into.

Why Invest in Property?

There are many reasons why investing in property in Australia makes very good sense now and in the future. The fundamentals which make investing in residential property so incredibly rewarding are summarized below.

Compound Interest

Compound Interest is the interest that is calculated on both the principal and the accrued interest. This is a very powerful law and it applies both rate and time to something. Eventually, it will reach a point called critical mass and this is where the growth is exponential. This is easily demonstrated in the below example:

If you doubled 1 cent every day for a month how much money would you have at the end of the month?

Value vs. Price

Real estate makes for one of the best investment vehicles due to the fact that the value and price can be very different if you know how to find these deals. What do I mean by that? If someone really needs to sell a property for whatever reason, you have an opportunity to get the property at a price that is far less than its value.

Average Growth Rate

Property prices on average in Australia have grown by 7% – 10% per year. This is an average growth rate which means in some years you might have 17% growth, while in other years you might have 1%. It depends on which part of the property cycle that particular property is in that year. Average can also imply that the property is an average performing property; there are areas where property prices have seen and average of 15% growth each year, it's just about understanding what makes an area experience this consistent growth and do the research from the right sources.

Rule of 72

The rule of 72 is a widely used formula to calculate roughly how long an investment takes to double in value - this formula is used in every asset class:

$$\frac{72}{\text{Interest (pa)}} = \text{Years to Double}$$

Add Value Potential

With property, there are many ways that you can easily add value to increase your equity, without waiting for natural (market growth). The best deals are done when you create or add your own value and have natural growth occurring at the same time.

Getting into Good Debt not Bad Debt

When you invest in residential property you have 3 sources of payment which is why it is good debt, as someone else is paying for most of it, if not all of it. The 3 sources are the tenant, the taxman, and yourself. Bad debt is when you have to pay for the whole amount of the repayments yourself and the item depreciates overall in value (like a brand new car or boat). Being in debt is great, if it's good debt!

Leverage

Leverage is the ability to control a large amount of money with a small amount of money. "Ever more, with ever less." Residential property is one of the most favourable investments for leverage, as the banks consider residential investment as a very safe investment; therefore they have the confidence to lend higher amounts against it. Here is an example of leverage:

Let's say that you have just inherited $200,000 and you decide to invest in real estate. In the first example you purchase a property for $200,000 (ignore the purchase costs for the examples), and let's assume that you bought in an area that experiences 8% average growth per year, after 10 years the property would be worth $431, 785.

Now, let's imagine that you used the power of leverage and you bought 2 properties in the same area (8% average growth per year), each worth $400,000 and putting down a $100,000 deposit for both and borrowing the remaining amounts (which makes that a 75% lend). After 10 years the properties would be worth a total of $1,727,140 which makes a total capital gain of $927,140. (See table, right)

Year	1 Property	2 Properties
0	$ 200,000	$ 800,000
1	$ 216,000	$ 864,000
2	$ 233,280	$ 933,120
3	$ 251,942	$ 1,007,770
4	$ 272,098	$ 1,088,391
5	$ 293,866	$ 1,175,462
6	$ 317,375	$ 1,269,499
7	$ 342,765	$ 1,371,059
8	$ 370,186	$ 1,480,744
9	$ 399,801	$ 1,599,204
10	$ 431,785	$ 1,727,140

Emotions

This applies to both buying and selling properties. There are many different situations that will involve people's emotions when investing in property. This is both good and bad when it comes to negotiating a deal. For example, if you are looking at a property to buy to live in and your partner says, "Oh I love this place", and the agent hears it, you are not in a good position to negotiate. Real estate agents are always on the alert for emotional buyers….

Shelter

This is the big difference between commercial and residential property investment. Everyone needs to live somewhere, so assuming you do your research and make an educated decision on your investments, you should never have an issue with an empty property.

Supply and Demand

The demand for certain properties in certain areas will always ensure good solid growth over the long term. It's important though to recognise the areas high demand now and in the future as there are areas that will not experience demand in the future.

Population

The population of Australia is growing both with the natural birth rate and immigrant population growth rate. Below is an extract from the Australian Bureau of Statistics illustrating this growth with the death rate and ageing population rate taken into consideration:

Population size and growth

Australia's estimated resident population (ERP) of 23.0 million people is projected to increase to between 30.9 and 42.5 million people by 2056, and to between 33.7 and 62.2 million people by 2101. Series A projects the highest growth, while Series C projects the lowest growth.

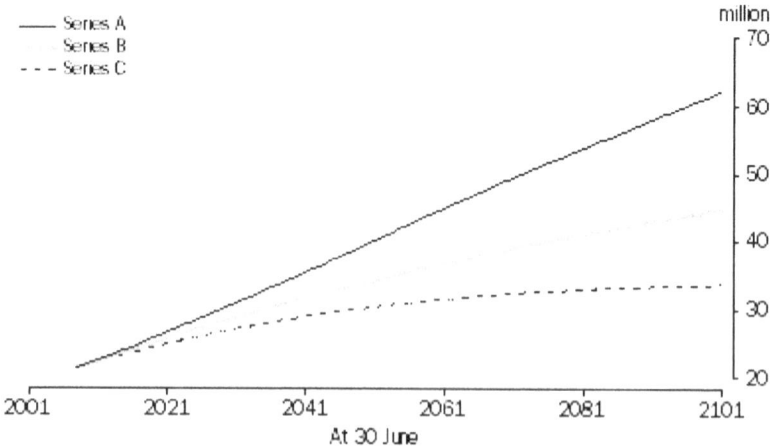

Insurance

Another major benefit of investing in real estate is that fact that you can insure just about everything against damage, theft, loss of rent, etc. It's best to seek a professional in the area to ensure that the right policy is in place for the property. There are some areas, however, that insurance companies will not insure due to the demographics and socio-economic status of the area, so it's a good idea to check this out as part of your due diligence. Note: It's always better to be over insured than under insured!

Tax Deductions

This is another advantage when investing in property, but it should never be the reason to invest in property; it's just an added benefit. You will need to speak to your accountant to find out what you can and can't claim, but in general, if it has anything at all to do with the property investment, you could claim it.

Depreciation

Property also has other benefits to consider when investing. Depending on the age of the property, you can claim the depreciating values of the fixtures and fittings as well as the raw construction costs of the building. Essentially, the newer the property, the higher the amount of depreciation you can claim against your taxable income.

These are also known as "on-paper losses" as it is not a physical loss out of your pocket that you are paying for, rather the loss is generated from the depreciating values of the building and/or items which makes it a loss on paper only.

The two ways that you are able to claim depreciation are the prime cost method or the diminishing value method. It's best to speak to your accountant regarding which type to use when claiming depreciation for your personal situation.

Generally speaking, depreciation is calculated in 2 parts:

The raw construction cost of the building – This is calculated by determining what the cost was at time of construction, so depending on the age of the property this figure will vary. The figure is then claimed at 2.5% over 40 years. Please note that if a building was constructed between 1987 – 1989, the depreciation rate for the construction costs are calculated at 4% instead of 2.5%. This was because is a change in government policy at the time.

Fixtures and Fittings – This part of the total depreciation calculation is only really valid for properties under 5 years of age. This is because most fixtures and fittings have a life span of 5 years therefore they are depreciated at higher rates. Depending on the item the rate ranges from 7% - 22%.

There are professionals that specialise in generating depreciation reports for your property and they are called quantity surveyors. For a small fee, usually of between $330 - $550, you can get a comprehensive report which they complete for you with every item captured, and the report lasts as long as you are depreciating the property (up to 40 years).

Note: Also be aware that if a property has had some improvements on the building there is a difference in the way you can claim the expenses depending on what you have done. If it's a "repair" you can claim a deduction for the cost immediately. A repair restores the property to the condition it was in when you bought it; the work must relate directly to the wear and tear or damage that occurred as a result of renting out the property.

If you are making the property better than it was when you first bought it, this is considered a "capital work" or "capital improvement" to the property and you can only claim the depreciation of the expenses over a period of time depending on the item.

Types of Property

One of the first things that new real estate investors ask is what type of property is best? Is it residential, commercial or industrial? The best advice I can give first and foremost is to get into whatever it is you're interested in. Don't listen to people who claim that wealth can only be obtained from a specific type of property. Or people who tell you to stay far away from commercial. The bottom line is this: all types of property can work, if you know how to work them.

Your job is to find the best deals; whether it's a $25,000 house, a $100,000 commercial building or a $300,000 apartment building. To start off, it's always best to start with properties that you are familiar with.

Residential Property

Residential real estate is an excellent way to build wealth. You buy and hold properties, pay off the debt, and watch the property's value appreciate. Below are some options under this category and their advantages and disadvantages:

Single-Family Homes

What about basic, single-family bread-and-butter homes rented to low- and moderate-income families? You do not need to have a lot of money to get into them; you can leverage out of them; you can buy them for less than what they are worth. They are in high demand, so they are fairly easy to rent and sell if you take care of them.

Advantages

- Easy to rent.
- Easy to sell.
- They appreciate nicely.

Disadvantages

- If you own a house and another house there on scattered sites, they become more difficult to manage and may cost you more to hire property managers.
- If you do not screen your tenants well, you may face late rent, plenty of repairs when they move out or tenants who end up not leaving before paying their rent.

Strata Title Schemes

Advantages

- Easy to rent. Easy to sell as well, but not as much as single-family homes.
- While you'll be responsible for the interior of the building, common areas are maintained by the management association.

Disadvantages

- High maintenance/management fees.

Small Apartment Buildings

Small apartment buildings are classified as buildings that contain between 5-100 units.

Advantages

- Excellent cash flow.
- You can hire one on-site manager to take care of all the apartments, since your tenants will all live in one place and not scattered around, like they would probably be with single-family homes.

Disadvantages

- The more apartments you have, the more repair/maintenance work and effort.
- It's harder to sell an apartment building than a house in a bad economy because it's an investment property.
- It's harder to get financing for an apartment building, but you can still expect anywhere from 60-80%.

Large Apartment Buildings

Large apartment complexes require a lot more capital but can be very rewarding.

Advantages

- Excellent cash flow.
- Easier to manage since all your tenants will be in one place.
- You can hire one on-site manager to take care of all the apartments, since your tenants will all live in one place and not scattered around, like they would probably be with single-family homes.

Disadvantages

- Difficult to sell in a down-market.
- Difficult to finance because they require much more than a small apartment building.
- Maintenance/repair can be costly because of numbers.

Commercial Property

Commercial real estate refers to strip centres, office buildings, industrial and commercial warehouses:

Advantages

- It is generally the tenant's responsibility to take care of any repairs, unlike residential property.
- Rent can be lucrative, especially for bigger areas.
- Commercial property in a hot location can see you fighting off the tenants!
- Less risk of losing a long-standing tenant in a downwards economy.

Disadvantages

- Usually harder to finance than residential real estate.
- Takes longer to find suitable tenants who want exactly what you're offering.
- Commercial property is harder to fill after it becomes empty in a down economy.
- With more and more businesses going only, less companies are looking for office space, especially in a downwards economy.

Land Development

- Land development refers to finding land, improving it with roads/utilities then selling it off for a big profit, either to a commercial or residential developer.
- "The two best businesses in the world are buying whiskey by the bottle and selling it by the shot, and buying land by the acre and selling it by the lot."

Advantages

- A land development gives you the potential for a tremendous profit because you are dealing with a bigger chunk of land.
- A land development will likely increase in value, especially if you improve it with roads and services.

Disadvantages

- The land cannot produce any income for you before selling it, so investors taking this route have to have real money.
- There are other associated costs you have to factor in after purchasing the land (taxes, insurance, mortgage, etc).
- Difficult to sell in a down economy.

Industrial Property

Advantages

- With industrial units, you are likely to get long term tenants, who are not likely to move out suddenly. Normally you will get three to six months' notice before the property is vacant.
- Tenants may also pay all outgoings such as water rates.

Disadvantages

- It may take a while for you to get a replacement tenant and while you wait, your holding costs will increase significantly.

Making Money with Property

Capital Growth Deals

So how do we identify above average capital growth areas? The best way to identify good capital growth areas for exceptional and consistent above average growth are summarised by the following 6 points:

1. Research and understand the demographics of the area. Particularly pay attention to the average income and see if that has been increasing over time. Also check for a high employment base in the area, and often where young working professionals are moving in.

2. Look for areas where physical land is in limited supply and demand is growing. It is also important to identify if construction of residential buildings in the area has slowed or cannot keep up with the growing population.

3. Areas that are known as popular areas where more people want to live. The increased consistent demand will put pressure on supply and therefore consistently increase prices.

4. Infrastructure that makes and area "attractive" or accessible. Such infrastructures include shopping complexes, schools, cafes, commercial buildings, parks, etc.

5. High and stable levels of employment; this is an important part for the consistency of growth. People prefer to live closer to work and therefore the area that is close to stable employment becomes very popular to rent, which brings me to my final point.

6. Higher yields cause high growth to occur in an area. When the rent continually increases there is added interest from investors to purchase in that area and also current tenants also decide they should buy. Both these factors cause increase demand and result in price growth.

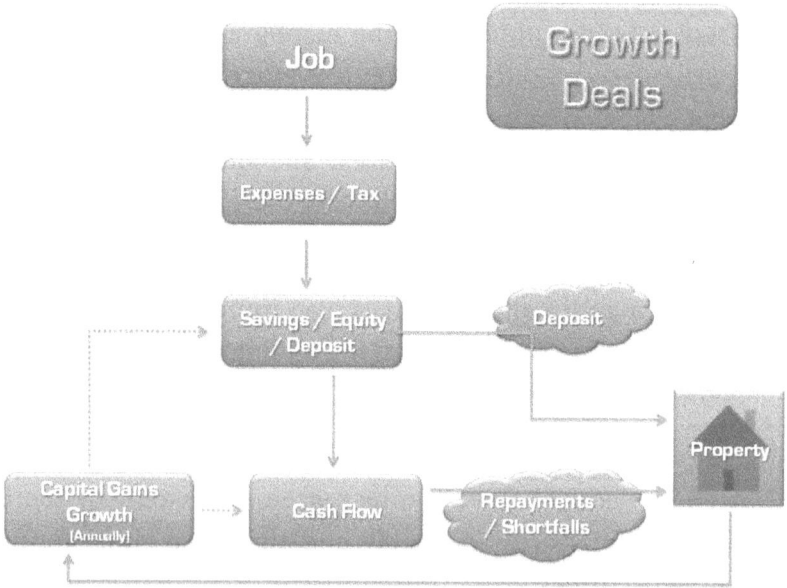

Cash Flow Positive Deals

The best way to determine whether a property is going to be a good cash flow positive investment is to use the following formulae:

$$\frac{\text{Weekly Rent (\$)}}{2} \times 1000 = \text{Purchase Price}$$

Or...

$$\frac{\text{Purchase Price}}{1000} \times 2 = \text{Weekly Rent}$$

These two formulae are the same, but the reason why I have shown you both ways to make sure that you think about cash flow deals in 2 ways:

1. Focusing on the purchase price in negotiations to identify a good cash flow deal
2. Focusing on increasing the rental enough to create a good cash flow deal

Example:

A property is for sale and is currently rented for $200 per week; calculate what purchase price you would have to pay in order for this property to be a good cash flow positive deal?

Answer is no more than $100,000.

$$\frac{\$200}{2} \times 1000 = \$100,000$$

Another way of purchasing a good cash flow positive property is to increase the rental income. You can do this by either finding out from the local agent what the property would rent for if you added a bedroom, or renovated it, or painted the house, etc.

Another easy way to increase your rental income is to fully furnish the property. You can use second hand furniture from garage sales, second hand furniture shops, and ads from the newspaper to totally furnish your properties that have the potential to instantly turn it into cash flow positive. You need to do your research to make sure there is a market for that particular type of rental in your area otherwise you will not see the increase. Ask your local rental agencies what they think and what the demand is like in that area.

Quick Cash Deals

These deals are great to use for a few reasons. When you're pre-purchase intention is doing a buy and sell, you are able to set yourself up correctly to support this from a taxation point of view, and know the calculation based selling numbers before heading into the deal. These are the sort of deals that are generally done in a boom. In general day-to-day, you've got to hunt further and hunt harder. Negotiation is usually how you create these deals in non-boom times. The harder you negotiate, the easier it will become.

These are the important areas to consider when deciding to do quick cash deal:

- Costs are very important, these costs include the entry and exit fees of the property, the actual costs involved for the value adding portion of the deal, and also the holding costs of the property. This is why it's so important to do your math upfront, as it can be easy to over capitalize and not make any profit at all.
- Timing is very important. As mentioned earlier these deals are best done in boom times; however you can still create fantastic quick cash deals at any time if you look hard enough and negotiate well.
- Buy well and add value.
- Councils – Only if you're doing deals which involve Development Permits/Applications. If so, you will need to allow for costs of the DA and the time it takes for council to process.

Some of the uses for doing quick cash deals are as follows:

- Increasing your current security position for your lending situation if you have existing properties which means lowering you're overall LVR.
- Getting a deposit together for your next/first purchase.
- Using the cash to pay down debt on another property to convert it into positive cash flow.
- Buying a new car, overseas holidays, diamonds etc.
- To live off as your income.

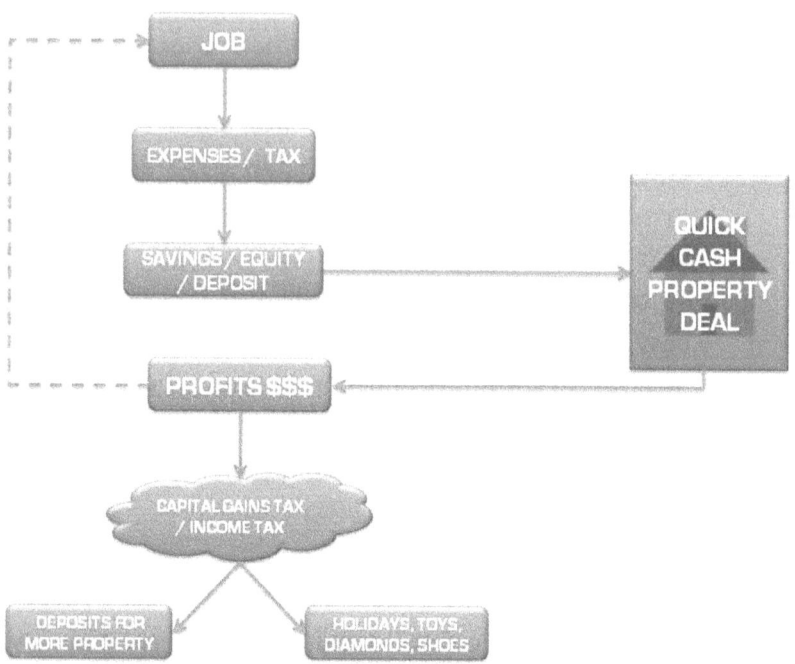

Subdivision

The most common reconfiguration of lots in residential property is Sub-Divisions.

Sub-divisions are used to "split" the land up into smaller lots. You will need to understand the zoning of the area before doing this as this will dictate the smallest block size allowed in the area. This strategy again requires a Development Approval process through the local council and is a bit more involved than the strata tilting unit's strategy.

It is very important to have a good team of experts around you to help you successfully execute a sub-division and they generally take longer to finish then strata titling.

I highly recommend that you get as much information as possible on the property before making any decisions – e.g. all services plan, zoning of property, drainage plans, any previous applications made on the property etc. The criteria to consider when conducting a feasibility of a sub-division are as follows (but not limited to):

- Sewerage – Location of closest manhole, the lay of the land and the depth of the sewerage pipes all have an impact on the sub-division. You may need to cross in to nearby neighbours' yards to connect into the sewerage system, which means you may need to pay for re-fencing, or re landscaping if it goes through a garden etc. (you will need permission from the neighbour to do this which is outside of council, so it's a good idea to be friendly with the neighbours and maybe offer them a "disturbance gift/fee".)

- Phone and Power – This will vary depending on type of block configuration and power supply (overhead/underground). It's best to speak with your surveyor about how you will get the services to the other block, but is it good to at least be aware that this will be required.

- Driveways – The council will often take advantage of a developer and get them to redo the front drainage/guttering on the road if it requires it. A concrete driveway will be required to the new allotment all the way to the front of the road.

- Stormwater/drainage – Depending on the slope of the land, re-levelling may be required as part of the development approval.

- Fencing – New fencing will be required for the new allotment and the council may require you to upgrade the neighbours fencing if applicable.

- Landscaping

- Crossovers (when adding a new driveway, this is the part that crosses the drain/guttering)

As you can see this is not something you want to rush into. Without the right information and team around you, it can cost you the project and consequently your cash. However, on the other hand, with some guided direction, information and willingness to work with the council, the profits can be very attractive. I have had both good and bad experiences with sub-divisions, and the biggest lesson from them all is to understand the council's local requirements and guidelines and the zoning of the property.

If you are not from the area where you want to do a sub-division, then I highly recommend hiring a town planner to assist with the approval process, then a project manager to complete the sub-division (one who has experience in managing these deals). This is an added cost to your project; however it is well worth considering, especially if you are not physically there and have no contacts in the area to rely on.

The 2 main types of sub-divisions styles are:

1. Corner block subdivision - type that allows street frontage for both lots once sub-divided (refer to corner block diagram).

2. "Battle axe" subdivision – type that splits the block in half behind the existing house, accessed by a driveway down the side of the existing house (refer to battle axe diagram).

Generally speaking, it is easier to sub-divide a corner block property, and the revaluation is typically higher if the new allotment has street frontage and is not behind the existing property.

Expenses to Consider

To subdivide a block into more than 1 lot requires consistent focus and attention to make it work in a relatively short amount of time. I have had experience in sub-divisions that took 12 months to complete, and others that took 4 months. This is not a strategy I would recommend anyone just starting out in small developments, due to the fact that there can be unknown expenses in the process (like replacing the entire sewer line in your property) and holding costs. Generally speaking, the council uses developers to pay for upgrading their services like drainage, gutters, sewer lines etc.

The costs to determine for these deals are as follows (but not limited to):

- Surveyors' Fees
- Council Fees (Applications, Permits etc.)
- Plumbing Works for sewer and drainage
- Electrical Works for new supply to lot (Including Application Fee to power authority)

- Fencing Contractor to erect new fencing and replace old fence if requested by council
- New Concrete Driveway for access to the new lot
- Cross over work - Drainage, guttering, concrete slabs etc
- Landscaping as required by council
- Fee for registering title - Department Natural Resources (DNR)
- Any additional work required from the council

Note: An important tip to remember if subdividing is to be in contact regularly with the council to find out where it is in the process. Once you submit an application, wait approx. 1 week then contact the local council to find out who the appointed assessing officer is for your application. Build rapport with them as soon as possible, get their direct number and email address if possible and maintain contact.

Once the DA (Development Application) has been approved, contact the council again to find out who the appointed field officer is and get their details as the council usually hands the application over to another person to continue the process. Also, put in the application for an operational works permit as soon as possible after the DA approval as this can take 2 – 3 weeks as well. During the process always ask the officer if there is anything you can do, or if there is anything missing from the application they will need, it's better to ask them then wait for the council to ask you, as this can delay the process significantly.

Buy and Hold

Buying and holding property in high growth areas is a good low-involvement strategy as:

- The compound growth and gearing effect multiplies your wealth immensely over time.
- You can become wealthy with this strategy while you continue your normal life, job, etc.
- The property will normally produce positive cash flow after a few years.
- You can use the build-up in wealth and equity to catapult yourself into your next property.
- Selling existing properties as well as looking for new ones is a time consuming exercise. The time you need to allocate to your investment is reduced by holding onto your existing properties. In fact, if you have a property manager, your involvement is really minimal.
- Entry and exit costs are also high – such as stamp duty, other purchase costs, mortgage entry and exit costs. Capital gains tax becomes payable on the sale rather than being deferred, meaning you often re-invest into a lower value property with less potential gain.

Below are the 33 steps you need to take to become wealthy through Buy and Hold properties.

- STEP 1: Complete your property plan to determine type of property and investment you want to undertake
- STEP 2: Assess your financial circumstances so you know the price range of your first investment property and identified financing sources

- STEP 3: Set up the most suitable structure for acquiring your properties
- STEP 4: Make sure your dream team is ready when needed
- STEP 5: Prepare/ raise the initial deposit and purchase costs
- STEP 6: Study the various areas in detail and decide on the area to invest in
- STEP 7: Start looking at your 100 properties in that area, talk to agents, understand the area and its pricing
- STEP 8: Identify properties that meet your criteria, do your desk research, and make appointments to inspect them
- STEP 9: Thoroughly inspect the interesting properties
- STEP 10: While on your field trip, look at comparables
- STEP 11: Decide on a property and asses its worth and your negotiation strategy
- STEP 12: Make an offer and negotiate the contract with agreed price and terms
- STEP 13: Conduct your due diligence
- STEP 14: Apply for and follow up on the finance
- STEP 15: Commission inspection reports as needed
- STEP 16: Pre-settlement inspection
- STEP 17: Settlement
- STEP 18: Before or after settlement (depending on the agreement), appoint property manager and commence tenant search
- STEP 19: Prepare the property for renting out
- STEP 20: Rent out the property

- STEP 21: Pay the mortgage and expenses, collect rent
- STEP 22: Carry out any maintenance work as needed
- STEP 23: Keep proper records and pay taxes when due
- STEP 24: Find new tenant if tenant leaves
- STEP 25: Watch the growth in the value of your property.
- STEP 26: When the value has gone up by 20 to 25% talk to your lender and do a formal valuation
- STEP 27: Start looking for another property using the same techniques and strategies
- STEP 28: Borrow the funds based on the increased equity of the existing property
- STEP 29: Use the borrowed funds as a deposit for a new property and borrow the balance secured on the new property.
- STEP 33: Repeat the process using several properties

Developments

In the buy and hold strategy, you have to wait for the appreciation in the value of the property to materialize through growth in property values over a period of time. Now in this strategy you do not have to wait. Instead, you actually add value to the property through renovation. You find a property that is in a poor condition, one that requires refurbishment, you renovate it and increase its value by an amount which is greater than the amount you spent on it.

The crucial issue in this strategy is the ratio of increase in value of the property in comparison with the total amount to be spent.

Return on cash invested is the best way to assess the viability of this strategy.

So basically, to assess the viability of a renovation project, we need to compare the total cash injection, including the deposit to buy the property and other expenses, to the overall increase in value of the property. Obviously, the greater this ratio the higher the more attractive is the investment.

I don't recommend major renovations for a buy and hold, as too much of your money goes into the building. If you plan to hold the property, it is better to buy properties that only need cosmetic refurbishment, at the most. Up to $20K (max $40K) and the property value needs to be higher than the property cost plus the refurbishment cost in order to be a sound investment. However, if it's a major renovation, it's normally too much to sell for a profit.

A major renovation would include a project like a room add-on, a complete bathroom overhaul that included the need for plumbing to be re-done, or other such projects involving serious work to electrical, plumbing or structural systems. These major renovations take quite a lot of money to complete without necessarily adding any value to the property itself. Cosmetic refurbishments are those renovations that add immediate value to the property, such as fresh flooring, new appliances and fixtures, energy-saving touches, and so on.

Finding the Right Renovation Properties

It is not always easy to find suitable property to renovate. The property must be in the right location and in the right condition.

Let's have a look at the location first. The area must be upcoming and popular, i.e. an area where people want to live. This is especially true if your strategy is to hold onto the property (just as you would for any growth property). Otherwise, the growth of the area helps, but it is not an essential part of this overall strategy. Essentially, though, you don't want to be buying in an area that people are moving out of for whatever reason, be it high crime rates, unemployment or lack of amenities and facilities. So when you look for a property for renovation, make sure you check the area as you would for any other purchase.

Most Important Make-Over Rooms

Kitchen:

- Renovations can range from just replacing cupboard doors and stove/oven to a complete new kitchen (flooring, countertops, sink, appliances, etc.)
- Watch the costs carefully and don't do a more expansive kitchen than the suburb and house requires

Bathroom

- May be as simple as new taps and extractor fan or as involved as retiling and a new vanity

So how do we find suitable renovation properties?

Here are five ideas for finding properties for refurbishment:

1. Gentrification:

Gentrification is the restoration and upgrading of deteriorated lower income urban areas with the movement to the area of middle-class or affluent people. These areas are usually ideally located near city centers and are ideal for the middle class population.

Gentrification is usually the result of concentrated effort by the local government that invests heavily in an area to solve what is usually referred to as urban decay. In an effort to reduce crime and improve the area, the local government spends a lot of money in these neighborhoods, improving the roads and infrastructure, the local facilities while adding new amenities and giving a facelift to the whole area. The local government also releases any land it has for development, encourages developers and offer incentives to those willing to invest.

At the same time, the area is experiencing demographic shifts, including an increase in the average income.

These areas usually start improving fairly quickly and rents start to go up, and the low income local residents start to move out as they find that the area is no longer affordable while the price of their homes have noticeably increased. So it is an ideal situation for them to sell and move to cheaper areas.

Gentrification is the ideal setting for this sort of strategy, as not only will you find that there are many properties available for renovation, but you will also find that prices in these areas are still very reasonable while starting to rise fairly rapidly.

You have to be careful, though, where you buy in these areas, as not all parts are likely to improve rapidly, and pockets of dilapidated and run down areas will remain depressed for a quite a while. So, be very selective and try not to buy too deep into the area.

2. Retirees:

Often times, the homes of many elderly folks who have lived there all their live will need extensive refurbishment and modernization, and you may well come across some of these homes in really good high growth areas. These are the ideal properties for this strategy, as they are likely to give a high return on investment.

3. Vacant Leases:

Properties that have been rented out for some time and have become vacant may be in such poor condition cosmetically that the landlord is no longer able to get a suitable tenant for it. Often, you will find that the landlord is only interested in renting out the property and is neither willing nor prepared to carry out any renovations.

4. Abandoned Homes:

Homes that have been abandoned for ages that are now offered for sale are often ideal for this type of refurbishment.

While you drive round, keep an eye out for these properties. Sometimes an abandoned property is not offered for sale and enquiring about it may either trigger its owner to either enter into negotiations with you or put it on the market.

5. Homes that could be internally subdivided:

You could do internal subdivisions to add value as well. For example, you could add value to a property by increasing the number of bedrooms. Three bedroom houses, for example, may command a premium as they are more in demand in a particular area. If you have a large bedroom in a two bedroom house, you can just divide it into two so you have a three bedroom house. If you do that make sure that the resulting bedrooms are not too small. Just be sure to keep all your subdivision work under the same structure, as that minimizes your costs.

Renovations To Avoid At All Costs

All refurbishment work can be done at a cost, but there are some renovations that must be avoided unless the property is in an outstanding location. The renovations to be avoided are:

1. **Properties subject to foundation movement or settlement:**

    While this type of work is very specialized and expensive, some lenders do not even lend on properties that are subject to settlement of the foundation, especially if the movement is still current. To assess if there is any settlement of the foundation, check if there are any cracks or obvious movement in the property – a crack that's deep and is apparent on both sides could be significant movement of the foundation which is quite serious and expensive to fix.

2. **Properties that are in extremely poor condition**:

    A property that has been fully gutted by a fire or one that's totally derelict is quite expensive to renovate. You not only have to start from scratch, but unlike building a house from new, you may also have to adopt certain construction techniques that are quite expensive.

3. **Properties that has been seriously infected or where all timber is badly rotted.**

    If the infestation or rot has spread throughout the house, then you have to rip everything out before you even start. This type of renovation is also very costly and is best avoided.

4. **Properties that contain hazardous material**.

    Some old properties may contain hazardous material, which is not usually a problem until you start taking things apart. A typical example is Asbestos. In the old days, Asbestos was used as an insulation material. This is a very dangerous material that must be removed by specialist Asbestos removal firms. This type of work is very expensive, and if in doubt, you should get an Asbestos report before you commit yourself to the property.

5. **Properties with structural damage.**

    In these types of properties, support structures and sometimes foundational work will have to be replaced. This requires a great deal of manpower, machinery, and cost. Any structural damage will be apparent in the home inspection.

Strategy Requirements

The amount of cash or the cash flow requirements to carry out this type of development very much depend on the extent of the work to be carried out on the property. So you should only consider following this type of strategy if you have enough cash available or a very strong cash flow and can afford to buy a property that can be renovated, can afford to do the work, and actually have the cash to cover all the costs and expenses that will be incurred along the way as many lenders may not lend you the funds to do the renovation. This is especially true if you are already borrowing near the limit to purchase the property.

The other requirement for this type of strategy is that you need to have time and dedication to carry out the renovation. This strategy is time consuming and requires that you spend a fair bit of time overseeing the work, talking to the trades people and project manager you have hired to complete the project, and following up on the progress of the work to make sure it is following your specifications.

Benefits of The Strategy

When you hold on to the renovated property, you're holding on to the property at the increased value and in so doing, you would get a better quality tenant because of your work that has been done on the property and you'll be able to get higher rental, significantly reducing any negative cash flow. You may even be close to a neutral gearing with this type of strategy. Needless to say, the property must be in a high growth area if you were to hold on it to as capital growth is the key to wealth creation in property investment.

The other benefit of this strategy is that it gives you more than one option. If you do not wish to hold on to the property, you may sell it off at a profit, generating some cash to carry out further projects or to support your existing high growth properties or to enable you to buy more high growth properties. The main factor you need to watch if you follow that strategy is to ensure that the market will enable you to sell the property at a reasonable profit within a relatively short period of time.

If you can find the right properties that will show a good return on capital, you are able to handle the renovations and have enough funds or a good cash flow to do the renovation work, then this is a great strategy that will generate cash for you and accelerate your investment growth and real estate wealth through adding value to your property within a short period of time.

Rent to Own

The rent-to-own strategy is best known for how it can help tenants buy a home before they're financially approved by traditional lenders. However, rent-to-own is a strategy that doesn't operate without private investors who are in a position to secure financing and partner with a tenant who has a higher-than-average risk profile.

While home ownership is a universal desire, tight lending rules send more people to alternative lenders, and open up opportunities for investors who are interested in high cash flow for the short term.

Rent-to-own basics

When you invest in a rent-to-own property, you're purchasing a property with a tenant in tow who, in the majority of cases, has helped select the property that they intend to buy at the end of a specified term.

In essence, you're helping to finance the property for a tenant who cannot receive traditional financing because of a few hiccups on their credit report. Over the course of the lease, the tenant pays above market rent to live in the home, while a portion of the rent goes in an "option fund" toward their down payment.

At the end of the agreed upon term, the tenant has the right to use the "option" to purchase if their credit has been repaired, and they can buy the home with the down payment saved in their "option fund."

Short-term benefits

So why would an investor go this route? For one, you're collecting above market cash flow on a monthly basis. Tenants generally pay 20 per cent above market rents. Secondly, it's a low-maintenance rental property because it does not require general maintenance, repairs or upgrades.

In that way, you're ridding yourself of any property management fees and nixing the traditional landlord-tenant relationship.

The flexibility of the contract is also a benefit. In most cases, you can write lease-to-own contracts any way you want. In some cases, the investor will lock in a certain value for the home based on where the market is currently, plus an annual appreciation rate (anywhere from four to eight per cent). In other cases, the investor doesn't lock in any price and it floats with the marketplace.

But in all cases, the contract will list a set time period for the term, at which point the tenant may purchase the home. If they're not quite there in terms of credit, the investor may choose to allow the tenant to continue to pay "rent" until they get there, or part ways – however, it should be predetermined in the contract what will happen in that event. And that event happens about 50 per cent of the time. For some people life changes and they recognize they're not in a position to follow through.

When to use this strategy

While the majority of rent-to-own transactions use the tenant-first strategy (ie. the tenant selects the property) as opposed to the property-first strategy (whereby the investor has a property he or she is looking to find a renter/buyer for), if the latter option is your preference, timing is key.

Rent-to-own is best used as a disposition strategy in weak markets. When the market is not favourable to selling, when it's very competitive and there are a lot of products on the market, use rent-to-own to differentiate yours from other inventory and to give your property a competitive edge in the marketplace.

Property Options

Stock market investors are familiar with options as they play a useful role in markets. They enable speculators and investors to take a position in a stock without the full outlay of buying the shares. A fund manager for example might be contemplating buying a large purchase of shares but is wishing to see their interim profit results before committing. Of course, if the results are above market expectations then the share price would probably rise. If on the other hand the results are below market expectations then the share price would fall.

Holding a call option over a parcel of shares gives the manager the opportunity to buy the parcel of shares at a fixed price within the period of the option expiry. If the manager does not exercise his rights to buy the parcel of shares by the due date, then the options will expire worthless and the manager has lost the money that the option has costs. However he will not be exposed to the losses that the entire parcel of shares would have experienced in the case of a share price decline.

In relation to property developer, in a similar fashion, a developer would not want to be exposed to the vagaries of the planning and approval process and seek to obtain an option over the desired property. He may also need to secure a number of adjoining sites – a process which is highly problematic and fraught.

A development approval from the local council allows you to develop the property and reap the benefits of the massive amount of value a developer can add to the property.

What are Options?

Definition: An option that gives the buyer the right but not the obligation to buy a property at a later date for a set price.

Reasons for using an option contract:

1. Secure a property to ascertain whether it is suitable for development without purchasing it.

2. Purchase a property off-the-plan and re-sell when it is completed.

3. Used a method to secure a property for a price in current market conditions and pay for it later when the price may have gone up.

4. Used as a method for rental/purchase. That is, rent the property for a period prior to purchasing it at some time in the future.

Options, in effect, allow developers to "lay by" a property and buy it at a later time if they wish to do so.

A Property Option is a legal instrument (a document) that allows you to control a property. With the property under control, it now allows a developer to profit firstly from the natural growth of a property, but more importantly it gives the developer the ability to add massive value to the property in the form of a Development Approval. A development approval is simply an approval from the local shire or council to develop your property, hence the value of the property goes up.

This ability to tie up a property pending the approval process clearly offers a value to the developer. If a DA is not forthcoming within the time frame then a developer can simply walk away from the deal. The developer's exposure is thus:

- The option fee
- Costs in relation to applying for a DA.

Option Fee

Options are one of the most powerful tools available to developers. They give developers the right to control a site during a set period of time, without the obligation of taking ownership, and usually with only a comparably small monetary risk. There is no standard formula for calculating the value of an option. In their use in the stock market, investors use highly sophisticated software to calculate the value of an option over an underlying security.

In stock options a number of variables are factored in to the algorithm including:

- Price of underlying security
- Strike or exercise price of option
- Historic price volatility
- Time to expiry.

All of these are relevant for the property developer too although the underlying volatility in the property market is much lower than the stock market. Also the principle factors in the property developer's situation are the current value when compared to the value of a completed development.

In the stock market option process are quoted publicly and can be traded on the market; in the property developer's case, the fee is worked out in the marketplace by negotiating what the buyer is prepared to pay – and risk if they don't proceed to and exercise their right to buy the property – and what the vendor is prepared to accept for taking their property off the market with no certainty of outcome.

The option fee can vary from nominal to thousands of dollars – it will usually be determined by the seller and be dependent on their aggressiveness in selling the property. If they have hopes of a fast sale a substantial fee will usually be requested to compensate them if they should lose a sale to another buyer.

The option fee is usually held by the seller. If the property is purchased this fee is generally not deducted from the overall purchase price.

Typically for residential developments for example duplexes, small villa developments and low rise developments, the fee can range from $1,000 to $10,000. The vendor would incur legal costs in having documentation vetted so their position would need to be attractive enough, after legal costs.

In the case of high rise developments or for commercial projects where the lead times are much longer and where the approval process can thus be longer, then fees can up to 5 per cent of the ultimate purchase price.

Advantages over contracts

The biggest difference to a Contract of Sale is an agreement between the buyer and seller of a property that spells out the costs and terms under which a sale will take place is that once exchanged a Contract of Sale is binding to both parties; an option is just that – an option for the buyer to go to a Contract of Sale after exercising the option.

Some of the many reasons that Option contracts are used by developers have included:

- they're low cost - only a relatively small amount of money is required to control the property
- the property is controlled without the downside of ownership, such as rates and other taxes, insurances, possible problems with tenants, etc
- they can be transferred or assigned to another party in the option period
- privacy is maintained

- cash is protected – rather than buying property with 100% of your cash, you only use a small percentage of your own funds
- limited risk/high return – options limit your risk while potentially giving a high return, using the leverage of a small option fee. Also if property prices drop significantly you do not need to exercise the options
- control the site without purchasing it - the advantages of controlling & not owning is, quick cash, no land lording, no monthly mortgage repayments, no property/land tax, no insurance, no maintenance costs, no potential lawsuits, no extensive record keeping & no income tax problems
- buys time to obtain the development permit application
- buys time to source financing – either to bring in a money partner, or put together the financing, or even to clean up and improve a poor credit record
- buys time to secure neighbouring property if they are integral to a development
- an option allows you the time to put together the necessary team or partners required for a successful project
- able to watch the direction of the market, especially in a fluctuating market, and decide whether the development is a good risk
- handle contingencies such as if you attempt to gain a zoning change and are unsuccessful you can choose not to exercise the option

- possible tax planning advantages, especially for the seller. I recommend you confirm with your own legal advisor regarding your particular circumstances, but usually an owner may enter into an agreement and exercise the Option to sell in different financial years thereby deferring their capital gains tax for another year.

Scenario

A developer wants to acquire a site which represents as a possible development of a number of town houses. The developer needs to negotiate with two land holders and to bring in several joint venture partners as well as seek DA approval when rights are obtained. He seeks a contract with a 3-month option period. The developers needed the option to allow them enough time to "round up" the numerous partners.

Options in the sale process

Options are also used as financial instruments by developers in the sale process in particular when marketing apartments off the plan. Here the options giver the unit buyer the right to buy the property but not the obligation, to buy the property at a later date for a set price.

Part of the appeal was that it was initially thought the buyer could avoid paying stamp duty on the apartment. As prices rose through 2002 and 2003, these call options became very valuable, and the race was on amongst investors, agents and developers to make as much profit from a rising and frenetic market.

The market has changed and in more recent times the option market over on-sales has quietened down as profits available to off the plan buyers have been highly subdued.

Lower stamp duty

On the issue of stamp duty, if a buyer acquires a property by the normal route of a Contract for Sale then stamp duty will be payable on the full value or purchase price of the property, whichever is greater. If an investor procured an option to buy a property and the option was on-sold for a profit, stamp duty would be payable only on the profit and not on the underlying purchase price of the property. This is highly beneficial to buying a property and on selling it where very large stamp duty would apply.

Amongst other advantages they can buy time for the developer – to complete their preliminary feasibility and planning to determine the projects financial viability and to even obtain the Development Approval/Permit. According to Robert Balanda in "Options Made Simple" they can even be used as an effective tax minimisation strategy.

An option contract also allows the luxury of tying up a property without having to settle on it, which is when your name is revealed in the public record as the buyer of the property. Walt Disney, for instance, assembled the Florida Walt Disney World site using options as he didn't want to reveal to the many different property owners that he was the intended purchaser, as they could have held out for a much higher price.

A downside with options is, that the money that is given as the option fee, is usually forfeited if the developer decides not to go ahead and does not purchase the optioned property. On the other hand the significant advantage of options is that the usually small option fee is all that is at risk.

The option agreement is usually attached to the contract of sale. Once the option is exercised a contract of sale becomes into effect. The contract of sale will detail the price and all of the necessary terms and conditions.

Disadvantages

> *"Well, real estate is always good, as far as I'm concerned."*
>
> ~ Donald Trump

The only real financial risk that a developer has, at this point, is the fee associated with the option and for any fees in relation to preparing an option agreement.

The main disadvantage of an option is simply, that most vendors have little or no experience in options and as such would not be interested in granting an option. It remains shrouded in some mystique and this is a deterrent to vendors. Here real estate agents have little to offer. Most have no interest in option deals and most do not really understand the process. In most real estate licensing courses it is not required knowledge.

There is no ready 'market' for properties over which sellers might grant a call option. You as the developer will have to source the vendors yourself. A vendor may be interested in entering a call option because they have attempted to sell without success. This may be an opportune time to give an inducement i.e. the fee to enter into an arrangement which may result in a sale.

The call option agreement will usually be subject to obtaining the development approval to add value to the property and this special condition may need the vendor to sign all application forms to the council.

There is a risk that approvals will not be forthcoming in the time of the option. This would mean either renewing (for additional fee) or lapsing the deal and walking away from it.

In order to win across a vendor to option the property, it would be prudent to keep the vendor informed. If as the developer you own the property, you are not accountable to another party in this fashion. This could be a verbal or written report on a monthly basis and would be a progress report in relation to the development process.

Capital Growth and Cash Flow

Capital Growth

Capital growth is briefly, the increase in the value of your properties over time – that will make you wealthy. To elaborate, it's an increase in value from investments that exceeds the purchase price, resulting in increased equity. This can be either natural (market growth) or manufactured (added value growth).

But there is a huge difference between 'high growth' and 'as long as I get a bit of capital growth, I'll be happy'. The difference is that the former makes you wealthy.

Growth potential is affected both by the area you buy in and the specific property you buy.

- **High growth areas:** If the <u>overall</u> increase in the value of property in an area is high, then it is a high growth area.
- **High growth properties:** Within areas, you'll find high growth properties and low growth properties.

There are several factors to take into account in determining whether an area or a property is high or low growth – not just the historical median price and average growth.

Look at the following example and see if you think it's worth a little extra effort to follow a proven system and buy the right property. The table and chart below look at two $300,000 properties growing at different rates.

- The first is a high growth property growing at 10% a year.
- The second is a low growth property growing at 4% a year.

If you think 'what's the big deal, it's just a few percentage points', take a look at this table:

	Property A High Growth	**Property B Low Growth**	**How much better is the High Growth?**
Yearly Growth rate	10%	4%	
Property value now	$300,000	$300,000	
Year	Property value after growth	Property value after growth	
5	$483,153	$364,996	$117,157
10	$778,123	$444,073	$334,050
15	$1,253,174	$540,283	$712,891
20	$2,018,250	$657,337	$1,360,913

- You can see that after 5 years the value of the high growth property has increased by $117,000 **more** than the lower growth property. That's **30% more**.

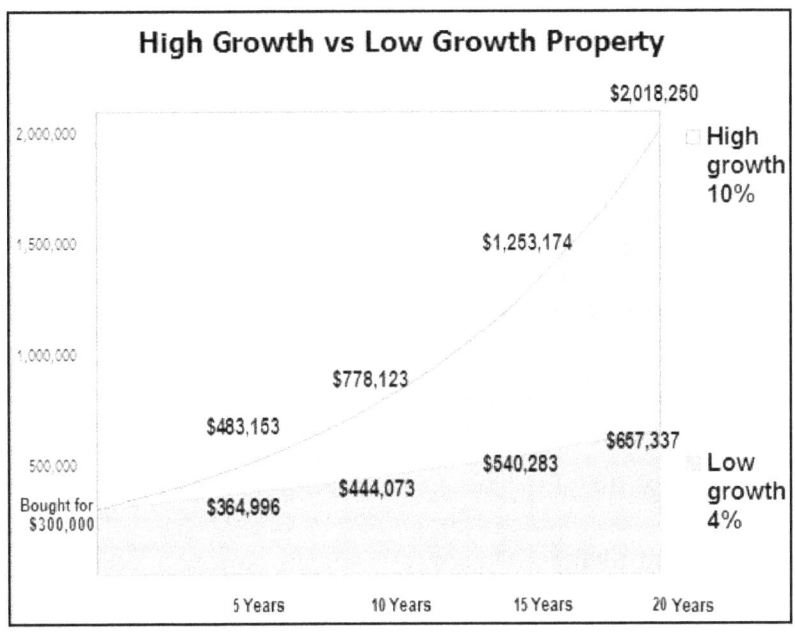

- After 10 years the high growth property has increased by $334,000 **more** than the lower growth. That's **75% more**.
- Now if you want to look further, the difference is over $700,000 after 15 years and over $1,350,000 after 20.

Choosing a high growth property instead of a medium or low growth one could easily be worth millions of dollars to you over time.

Cash Flow

The cash flow of your property will depend on your 'gearing' – i.e. how much of the purchase price you have borrowed – and on the property's rental income and expenses.

There are two main types of gearing:

- **Positive Gearing:** The monthly income is more than enough to cover the costs so you have a bit left over.
- **Negative Gearing:** The monthly income is less than the costs so you need to pay some of the costs out of your own pocket.

If the monthly income is exactly the amount needed to meet the monthly costs, this is known as Neutral Gearing.

Why Negative Gearing can be Great!

You're probably wondering why on earth you'd want to buy a property with negative gearing or negative cash flow. Well, it's important to point out that negative gearing isn't the reason people choose this investment. Let's look at a quick example of two different properties.

- ➢ Both of these properties were purchased for $300,000 (mortgage was at 80% so $240,000).
- ➢ Both of these properties have annual costs of $22,000 (interest is $18,000 at 7.5% and $4,000 for other costs).
- ➢ Now, the rental for each property is different. See the table below:

	Annual Rental	Annual Expenses	Annual Cash Flow	Gearing
Property A (Rental = 8% of Value)	$24,000	$22,000	+$2,000	Positive
Property B (Rental = 5% of Value)	$15,000	$22,000	-$7,000	Negative

Here, you can have a pretty good idea of where your income is more than your expenses—positive gearing. Where your income is less than your expenses, the gearing becomes negative.

How you can turn negative gearing into positive cash flow:

The actual cash flow looks slightly different in practice as some of the expenses incurred in owning the property can be set off against your taxable income.

The costs that can be set off against tax include your loan interest, some of the running costs and some 'depreciation'. Depreciation is an allowance that is made for the fact that the buildings and appliances decrease in value each year – as mentioned in the previous section. This means that your tax bill could be reduced by more than the amount of the shortfall.

Example

Shortfall on a property with negative gearing	$2,000
Depreciation and running expenses set off against taxable income reduces tax by:	$3,000
Negative gearing becomes a positive cash flow of:	$1,000

Now, that's useful to know but definitely not the sort of money you're expecting to make, is it? I think by this point, you've realized that having a positive cash flow isn't the answer to making you wealthy.

One point to bear in mind is that you should never buy a negatively-geared property just to take advantage of the tax benefits. You should always make the purchase based on sound investment reasons.

People often refer to positive or negative 'cash flow' as being the situation after tax benefits have been taken into account, whereas positive or negative 'gearing' refers to the surplus or shortfall between income and actual cash expenses. However this is not a strict definition. I will use the terms positive/negative cash flow and positive/negative gearing interchangeably.

Why some properties have negative gearing

Now, if you're wondering why some properties have a positive gearing, while others are negatively geared, the answer is quite simple.

Usually positively geared properties have a positive cash flow because of low capital growth. This happens because the value of your property hasn't grown as quickly as rents have increased,

- The price of the property is low in relation to the rent.
- The value of the property has stayed low because of low capital growth.

On the other hand, properties which have been growing in value are more likely to be negatively geared. This means that buying property that is growing in value is likely to involve negative gearing. Let's put that in context by considering the previous properties in the previous example:

Comparison: Positive Cash Flow vs. Growth Properties

In the example, each property has the same annual costs but different rental incomes.

	Purchase Price	Annual Expenses	Tax saved: up to	Annual Rent Income	Annual Gearing
Cash Flow Property A	$300,000	$22,000	-	$24,000	+$2,000
Growth Property B	$300,000	$22,000	$4,650	$12,000	-$5,350

If you're on a high income, we can also incorporate the tax savings:

	Purchase Price	Annual Expenses	Tax saved: up to	Annual Rent Income	Annual Cash Flow
Cash Flow Property A	$300,000	$22,000	-	$24,000	+$2,000
Growth Property B	$300,000	$22,000	$4,650	$12,000	-$5,350

Property A earns you $2,000 a year, while the 'holding cost' for property B is $5,350 a year.

So which of these properties is the better investment? You can't tell without looking at capital growth and taking into consideration your strategy.

So, let's look at how growth affects this equation. Assume Property A went up in value by 4% and Property B went up by 10%.

	Purchase Price	Capital Growth %	Capital Growth $	Value After 1 Year
Cash Flow Property A	$300,000	4%	$12,000	$312,000
Growth Property B	$300,000	10%	$30,000	$330,000

So just looking at capital growth, Property B looks a lot better.

But of course we have to look at both capital growth and cash flow together.

	Purchase Price	Capital Growth	Cash Flow	Net Position After 1 Year
Cash Flow Property A	$300,000	$12,000	+$2,000	$14,000
Growth Property B	$300,000	$30,000	-$5,350	$24,650

When you look at capital growth and cash flow together, you are better off owning property B after one year, despite the negative cash flow or gearing.

As time goes on, this difference becomes even greater (assuming the same costs and growth rates):

- After 3 years, you'd be more than $37,000 better off with property B.
- After 10 years, you'd be more than $220,000 better off with property B.
- After 20 years, you'd be more than $1 million better off with property B.

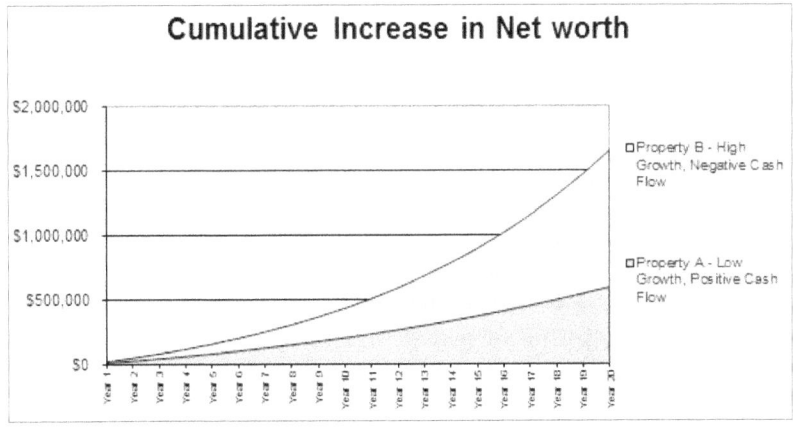

Who is the obvious buyer of cash flow positive property?

Both young people making a start in adult life and those nearing retirement may have a natural affinity to this form of real estate investing in favor of negative gearing. Young people starting out are not normally high income earners and would be attracted to the lower capital entry point on cheaper high-yielding low-growth properties. As people move into higher incomes they could look to higher-growth, low-yielding property, as they have the income to support it.

Similarly, as people get closer to retirement, and they plan for a cessation of job income, they find the bricks-and-mortar security available in higher-yielding properties appealing: yield that will give them the income for retirement. Rental income in retirement is an ideal solution as it offers capital preservation and an income that is closely linked to cost of living increases.

A Checklist for the positive cash flow property investor:

Because regional economics are such a critical factor that determine both rental yields and vacancy risk, investors ought to know answers to the following questions for each project:

- ✓ Is the residential population increasing, static or reducing?
- ✓ Are property values surging, stable or plummeting? (HINT: Take a three-year and a 10-year trend view).
- ✓ Are building approval numbers increasing, stable or falling?
- ✓ Is the demand for rental accommodation high, average or low?
- ✓ Are employment opportunities good, average or poor?
- ✓ Are the economics of the area positive, neutral or negative? (HINT: what is the trend on vacancy for retail or commercial property?)
- ✓ Are local services, for example, education, community services, transport; good, average or poor?
- ✓ Are tourist numbers increasing or decreasing?

- ✓ How do lending institutions regard local area? Do they apply a lower LVR ratio for the area?
- ✓ Is there a dominant industry in the area that could be subject to an interruption and which could then result in people leaving the district? Or is the local economy highly dependent on a single commodity such as wool, beef, or a particular mineral (coal, iron ore, sugar cane, etc).

Capital Growth vs. Positive Cashflow

The Myth

During the property boom – when prices in general were increasing rapidly – many people believed that positive cash flow properties were growing in value just like the rest.

That doesn't generally happen because the very reason these properties have a positive cash flow is that, while the rent may have gone up with inflation, the value of the property hasn't grown as much.

The prices may be increasing but they are not increasing as much as properties in other areas. We'll look at the factors that drive growth in property prices for different areas a little later but the main point is that high growth properties have more (or stronger) factors combining to push their growth.

In the property world, capital growth and positive cash flow are almost contradictory! They don't go together unless you can:

- Find a positive cash flow property that's located in an area that remained cheap for a long time, and
- You have done comprehensive research and you're very confident that something major is going to change the area which will generate a huge demand, and

- This demand cannot be met with the existing or planned supply.

These factors together could bring an abrupt and rapid increase in property prices. In that case, and as long as you've done a thorough analysis, you can conclude that you have a unique opportunity, but they are very few and far between.

Cash Flow vs. Capital Growth — a balance of both

Cash flow or capital gain? This remains the perennial questions at many a dinner party. The tax system in Australia produces a bias towards people gearing up: capital gains tax concessions combined with negative gearing and depreciation allowances bias individual investors towards property.

Yet common sense says that the less cash you need to fund your investment the better off you are.

The fact is that property investing is a dynamic activity: at some point you may be both making a loss in terms of cash flow while at the same time building capital value. Indeed if you consider property investing as a long term undertaking then it would be wise to have a pragmatic view: like any business activity, profits may not be forthcoming in the first few years; it is wise to expect that on top of the purchase price you usually need to invest some working capital to fund the 'business activity'.

As prices move up, buyers are attracted by the prospects of quick profits. Rising house prices puts the squeeze on rental yields. Simply put, rental yields cannot rise as rapidly as home prices when boom conditions are prevailing. At those times in the cycle, cash flow in fact may get tighter, as interest rates increase.

What investors want is that total return on a year-on-year basis makes several years of negative cash flow from the property investment relatively insignificant when calculated over the entire investment period. .

Tax matters

Positive cash flow investing means that you have more money coming in from a rental property than is going out.

Positive cash flow investing can arise from a negatively geared property:

The positive cash flow investment formula:

Rent + tax refund   greater than   interest + expenses = positive cash flow.

So, which is riskier?

Whatever the strategy of the investor – capital growth or rental yield, the fundamental rules of property investing call for a considered view to take into account both historic and possible capital growth in a particular area, taking at least a 10-year perspective. What's the average capital appreciation (over past 10 years)? What's the rental yield? Look at total return: a 6% rental yield and a no-growth situation do not make sense.

Buying in Mining Towns

Are Mining Towns great investments?

You probably know someone who has bought property in a mining town and made a small fortune out of it. Years ago, when everyone thought mining towns were bad investments, there were some crazy risk-takers who decided that it was worth the risk. It wasn't a huge risk, though, I mean, some people could buy a property within their credit card limits, so most people thought, hey, what's the worst that could happen? Stories abound about how so many people made a fortune from mining towns. But is it all good?

What is it about mining towns that causes property investors to lose their minds and ignore any risks to buy into mining towns? There are some pros and cons to mining towns just as there are in any other type of investment. Firstly, ALWAYS do your due diligence and make sure you know what you're buying. Some people think all property is good, and even if it's not particularly good right now, if they sit on it long enough they'll surely strike gold. If you sit on a property for ages, you could very well pay a small fortune in expenses. That's why it's important to do your research thoroughly. There are a lot of long-term property investment options, but these too are thoroughly researched and determined and studied. You can't just blindly walk into something hoping for the best.

The biggest downside of buying in mining towns is that the markets are more fragile and open to greater risk. For instance, if an industry shuts down, a local housing market can see its demand shrink massively very quickly. High rents stop, so do sales and property values drip.

Now, because risks are higher…the returns are better too and this is the biggest pro of this type of strategy. I suggest these markets great for people who like higher risk, or have other investment homes in more traditional markets and want to mix it.

Financing

Some people find that the main stumbling block in building wealth through property investments is raising the initial cash for the down payment. But you shouldn't let this common stumbling block stand in your path to real wealth. There are many possibilities that you could explore, and chances are good that at least one of them will work for you. Raising money might sometimes be difficult and may take time, so be patient and do not give up. Remember: only those that persevere will get what they want.

First, How Much Do you Need?

Before you can seriously start looking at properties, you need to have a clear idea of how much you can afford to spend. There is obviously no point in looking at properties or areas that are outside your current budget. So, before we look at your financing options, let's work out approximately what you'll be able to afford.

There are three elements that will determine how much you can spend on a property:

- How much you can **borrow**.
- How much **upfront cash** you have available to pay the deposit and other purchase costs.
- How much **weekly cash** you have available to cover any shortfall between the costs and your rental income.

As we go through each of these steps, you'll be able to see what you can buy.

Step 1: How much money can you borrow?

You can use one of these sites for an initial estimate of what you can borrow based on your income, but you'll need to talk with your mortgage broker for an accurate assessment:

http://hlc1.westpac.com.au/hlc/hlc/BorrowingPowerStart.do
http://money.ninemsn.com.au/property/tools/borrowing-power-calculator.aspx
http://hlborrowingcalc.webcentral.com.au/calculator.asp

> Fill in here the amount you can borrow based on your income.
>
> The amount I can borrow: $..

Step 2: How much cash do you have available for deposits, purchase costs, adding value, etc.

To establish how much cash you have available for the deposit, purchase costs and other upfront expenses, add up all the money you will be able to draw on from savings, selling other assets or from parents etc. Only include the amounts you want to use for your property investment.

Remember you will be committing this money into the property so it has to be cash you can have access to when you want to buy the property and which you can tie up in the property for some time.

Source of cash (e.g. savings account, parents, etc)

_____	$ _____
_____	$ _____
_____	$ _____
_____	$ _____
Total cash available	$ _____

> Fill in here the amount of cash you have available.
>
> The amount of cash I have available is: $............................

Step 3: How much equity do you have available for deposits, purchase, costs and adding value, etc.?

If you plan to use the equity in another property to fund your deposit, purchase costs or add-value costs instead of or as well as cash work out how much equity you have available here.

NB For an accurate assessment, you're better off working this out with the help of your mortgage broker as your income may still limit the total amount you can borrow even if you have a lot of equity.

Fill in the details of properties you own and here to estimate how much equity you have available to borrow against. Only fill in the properties that you want to borrow against for your property investment

	Property	Outstanding mortgage	Monthly payment	Estimated value	Estimated equity (mortgage - value)
1					
2					
3					
4					
5					
TOTAL					

This will enable you to determine the total outgoings and the equity that you have in your properties so you can determine how much more you can borrow against that equity.

For example, if your outstanding mortgages are $350,000 and your total estimated value is $750,000, then you estimated equity is : $400,000.

You can borrow against that equity to fund property purchases. So, if you want to borrow at a LVR of say 85%, then 85% of $750,000 means you can borrow up to: $637,500. You have already borrowed $350,000, so you can borrow another $637,500- $350,000= $287,500 which you can use as a down payment for your next property purchase

> Fill in here the funds available by drawing on existing equity in your properties.
>
> The funds available are: $..

Step 4: How much do you have available every week for holding costs?

Even if you will be renting out your investment properties, sometimes the rental you receive will not be enough to meet the loan repayments. This applies especially with many growth properties. It's important that you know exactly how much extra cash you have available EVERY WEEK to meet any shortfall.

My after tax income per year		$ _____
Less: My expenses per year		
Rent	$ _____	
Mortgages	$ _____	
Loans/Credit card	$ _____	
Food	$ _____	
Living Expenses	$ _____	
Utilities	$ _____	
Car/Travel	$ _____	
Medical	$ _____	
Other		$ _____
Other		$ _____
Other		$ _____
Total Expenses		$ _____
How much I have left per year		
To support my growth properties		$
Divide by 12 to give amount per week		$

> Fill in here the amount of cash you have available each week.
>
> The amount I have available each week is: $........................

This amount should be more or less the same as the money you actually have left over each week or what you save or what you currently just spend on unnecessary items that aren't on your list and you are quite happy to give them up. If your calculated amount is much more than what you believe you have left, you've probably left some expenses off your list.

If you don't have anything left over, you'll have to either

- **Reduce your expenses**: Go through your expenses in detail and see what you're willing to give up creating your wealth.
- **Increase your income**: You could work a few more hours a week or get a part time job.

This amount you've worked out is the maximum you can carry in 'holding cost', which is the shortfall between income and expenses of a growth property. It is the cost you pay to buy your wealth.

In calculating this number, be conservative. You should build in a buffer in case of unexpected costs or events.

Once you've checked your estimates, and you know what your excess is, start saving this amount every week now. This will help build up your buffer and help you check that your calculations are correct.

> **You now have an approximate idea of:**
>
> How much you can borrow based on your income $_____
>
> How much upfront cash you have available $_____
>
> How much you can borrow against your equity $_____

1. Equity

Assess the equity that's already available in your own home and use it to raise finance.

Many people don't realize that there is a lot of equity in their home, and now is the time to use it. Deduct the value of your home from the outstanding mortgage to see how much equity you have. You could start by having a discussion with your existing lender about a loan based on the equity that you have in your home, as that would be the easiest way of doing it since this lender already has a mortgage on the property. You may be able to borrow up to 95% of the value of your property, so if your home is worth $450,000 and your outstanding mortgage is $250,000, and you decide to borrow 85%, then you can borrow:

($450,000 x 85%) - $250,000=$132,500

If you made your mortgage payments on time, and you qualify on other criteria (such as your income), your existing lender should easily lend you the money. If you they won't, talk to your mortgage broker who will help you find alternative lenders.

2. Joint Ventures

Bring in a partner (or partners) who have the cash you need.

If you have someone you trust and can work with, why not introduce a partner or several partners? Both parties will need to have confidence that you have a solid plan. These partners can either lend you money at an agreed rate, or they can be the type of partner that has a share in both the risk and in the profit of the property.

3. Borrowing

Borrow the money you need from close family or friends.

Borrowing from family and friends is not as easy as it may sound. You have to be well prepared when you talk to them, as even if they are close family members or friends, their approach to financial matters could be completely different to the way you normally deal with them. It is best to have a written agreement drawn up here, as well.

4. Liquidating

Sell any belongings that you do not need or use.

If you have any valuable items that you no longer need or use, this is the time to sell them. Remember, you are selling to invest in something that's going to make you very wealthy, so even if you're perhaps emotionally attached to an item, like that old motorbike, classic car, or caravan that has been sitting there collecting dust, now is the time to sell.

5. Loans

Get a long term personal loan.

Getting a personal loan based on your income could be quite easy, especially if your credit history is good, but whatever you do, make certain that you do not take on loans with excessive interest rate or charges. Also, be sure to repay any personal loans as quickly as possible, as they will have a higher interest rate than your mortgage will have.

6. Classic Saving

Start saving from your current income.

Yes, this may be a long process, but cutting down on your expenditures and putting money to the side every month is a real start. In the meanwhile, you could be trying any of the other ways suggested above.

While you're raising money make sure that you are able to afford any repayments. Work it out and remember that not only do you have to service payments that become due on the money that you have raised for the deposit and purchase costs, but you will also have cover any negative cash flow that arises from the shortfall between the rental income and mortgage payments and other expenditures of your new investment property. Work out your expected rental income, mortgage payments and other expenses and check if you can afford it. You may find that the rental income alone will not cover all these expenses, as you'll be buying in high growth areas where properties are expensive and are, therefore, likely to produce a negative cash flow.

If you find that it's tight or you cannot afford it, reduce the amount of the loans and go for a smaller property. It's better to build it up gradually rather than borrowing as much as you can and then running into problems when you are not able to meet the various repayments.

Structures

Wealth protection is a strategy in which assets or wealth is protected against risk. What are the types of these assets? They can be in the form of a family home, a car, a business, a share portfolio, an investment real estate, valuable artworks, and many more. Who are the people who need this protection strategy?

There are four major groups:

- The very wealthy
- Those in the public eye who are prime targets for litigators and regulators
- People who own a business and/or engaged in a professional occupation
- People who suspect they might be a future target of legal, financial or even medical difficulty

Why do you need a wealth protection strategy? Because they act as shield against any crippling government penalties you may incur in the course of business, claims by an ex-wife or de factor partner, claims by disgruntled business associates/employees, and claims arising from an incident which caused a person to suffer a serious illness.

Here's one way of looking at asset protection: You're in a bitter litigation fight with an ex-partner who's suing your ass off for half of the business you put up together. This ex-partner, however, might give pause if he sees the barriers you've surrounded your assets with to protect it.

The asset protection serves as an obstacle your ex-partner must jump over before he can get his hands on your business. He sees this obstacle and he might be encouraged to settle favourably instead of getting involved in a long and drawn-out litigation process.

> ➢ **What you could lose**

Picture this: if you lose in a successful legal claim, liability action or bankruptcy case creditors will get their hands on your assets. The banks will have a field day disposing of your income, including your superannuation pension if any. Even if your claim is successful, it can be costly and a no win situation for you and your assets.

> ➢ **Who's at risk?**

Everybody from directors, executives and small business owners are open to legal action from disgruntled employees, competitors, suppliers, debtors and the ATO under the Trade Practices Act, Corporation Act and income tax acts.

Professionals and tradespeople alike can face multi-million dollar claims. Sole traders are personally liable for the debts of their businesses, and must meet any liability or professional negligence claims made against the business. Even as a partner in a business, you are individually responsible for all claims made against the business.

Property owners, motorists and people who employ domestic staff, such as cleaners and gardeners, are now frequently subject to Workers Compensation, liability and negligence actions following accidents.

> **Ongoing risks**

Another thing, your legal liability does not end when you sell your business/ property even when you retire since they can be put at risk by claims arising from actions or events that happened many years ago.

There are many ways to protect an asset or wealth but like a portfolio, they should be diversified and not dependent on one method alone. Here are some ways to consider:

- **Transfer your assets to your spouse**

This is not advice and should not be relied upon but in general the most practical way to protect your wealth is to transfer some of your assets to the name of your non-exposed spouse. In most cases, this generally means unencumbered assets like the family home. If the wife's name does not appear in any leases, and she has not signed any personal guarantees for trade debts, then the house is safe if the husband goes bankrupt.

A recent amendment to Australia's Bankruptcy Law, however, may put a damper on the effectiveness of this practice. Under the amendment, if the family home is in the wife's name and the husband goes bankrupt, the family home is still made vulnerable to a creditor attack unless the wife can prove she is meeting mortgage payments on the home from her own separate income.

Another thing to consider is what happens to the property if the spouse dies. In most cases, the asset automatically reverts back to the spouse's name and the heirs, barring some exemptions, may have to pay heavy stamp duty for its transfer.

- **Trusts**

Not many people can differentiate between a Trust and a Will. The main difference between the two is the manner in which your property is being disposed of after your death. In a Will, property goes on probate (court system) to determine its legalities and the properties being distributed. The property may also become vulnerable to taxes and legal fees.

In a Trust, the property is transferred to a Trustee, whether an individual or corporation, while you are still alive and will continue after your death. Under a Trust, the property will avoid probate and may be shielded against heavy taxes, creditors, and divorce claims when you die. It also means you no longer own this property but it is owned by the trustees of the trust. . You can, however, still have access to it in your lifetime and even instruct your Trustees who to leave it to after you die.

The trustee is the actual legal owner of the trust property since he is tasked to carry out its wishes. Trustees can also benefit from the trust. Trusts are generally cheaper than most alternative options to set up and no more costly to administer.

Trusts are advantageous since they can offer limited liability and income splitting possibilities for the beneficiaries and unit holders. Trusts have an 80-year life span, and all income must be distributed each year to avoid high tax rates.

Beneficiaries in a trust are generally classed into three types:

- Specified beneficiaries whom the trust was specially created, e.g. parents and children
- General class of beneficiary, which includes close relatives of the primary beneficiaries
- Tertiary class of beneficiary includes other trust or company in which the beneficiary has an interest

There are up to eight types of trusts. Here we will focus on the most common.

1) Discretionary Trust

Commonly referred to as a *family trust*, this trust is often the preferred structure in asset protection strategies because it is the trustee who must be sued and not the individual beneficiaries or other associated persons. Where the trustee is a corporate entity then the *"owners"* of the trust are usually fully protected from creditor claims against the trust by the corporate veil. A corporate trustee can therefore provide better asset protection to the individuals establishing the trust than would be afforded if they were to be trustee's in their own right. The distribution of income also provides a distinct tax advantage since it usually allows income to be distributed among the lower tax earners and even children, subject to the some limitation.

The discretionary trust, however, is generally not appropriate when trading or rental losses are expected. This is because they are quarantined within the trust and not available to be distributed to beneficiaries. Because of this, the trust may not be suitable for investors who apply negative gearing, unless income is also collected from other sources within the trust.

> *Success seems to be connected with action.*
> *Successful people keep moving.*
> *They make mistakes but don't quit.*
>
> ~ Conrad Hilton

```
                    Mr Jones        Mrs Jones
                          Directors
    Risk Protection ═══════════════════════════
                     Jones Family Pty Ltd
                           Trustee
                      Jones Family Trust
                         Beneficiaries
            Mr Jones   Mrs Jones    Jones Children
```

Mr. and Mrs. Jones and their children receive income from the Family Trust as determined by the trustee. That entitlement can change each year at the discretion of the Trustee depending meaning the taxation outcome can be optimized as circumstance change over time.

2) Unit Trust

Unit trust involves beneficiaries (called unit holders) owning certain shares (called units) in a trust. Under a unit trust, unit holders are entitled to income and capital distributions from the unit trust on the number of units they own in the trust. Trustees can also generally own units in the unit trust.

Unit trusts work because people outside your family can own units, borrow money and run the business anytime. The trust, however, is not flexible especially in the distribution of income, which is pre-determined by the entitlements of unit holders. . This can be modified but will often trigger capital gains tax issues.

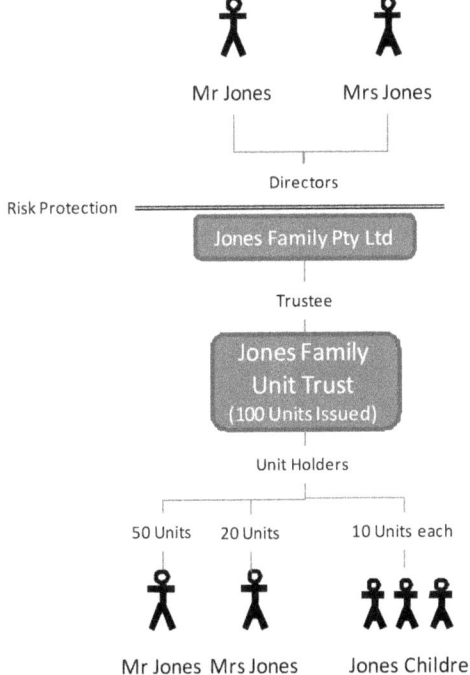

3) Hybrid Trust

Hybrid trusts combine the elements of both unit and discretionary trusts. In a hybrid trust, the trustee pays a certain amount to beneficiaries which are fixed by the settler. The trustee is allowed to make both income and capital distributions to beneficiaries in ratio to the number of units they own. Beneficiaries then can claim tax deductions for items like interest on borrowing, which allows this type of structure to be used in negative gearing situations.

Generally, hybrid trusts are good for asset protection, 50% capital gains tax relief, and estate planning benefits. They become disadvantageous, however, if they're not correctly established or run since they inevitably become unprotected and tax-challenged by the Tax Office.

4) Asset protection trusts

It's not unheard of for wealthy individuals to transfer a portion of their assets into an offshore trust to protect them from creditors and shield the assets for their children.

Besides the Cook Islands and Nevis, popular asset protection trusts are found in several American states including Alaska, Delaware, Rhode Island, Nevada and South Dakota. You may not need to be a resident of these states to set up an asset protection trust. However, you need to study the state laws carefully since one of the requirements of this type of trust is that it must be irrevocable and the laws can change.

Other requirements for an asset protection trust may include:

- The trust must have an independent trustee, whether an individual, bank or trust company licensed in that state.
- It allows distributions at the trustee's discretion.
- It should include a spendthrift clause.
- Some or all of the trust's assets should be located in the trust's state.
- All documents and administration must be in the state.

These trusts are the most expensive to establish and maintain and are generally only appropriate in specific situations.

Less Complex Ways to Protect Assets

The following are other inexpensive ways to protect your assets:

- Try funnelling more money into your employer-sponsored retirement plan, the tax benefits could be endless
- Hold member entitlements in SMSF's in a reserve account rather than in the members' entitlement account.
- Consider licensing high value assets so they are not directly owned by the entity exposed to the risk.
- Invest in insurance that gives shelter against personal-injury claims
- Take advantage of laws regarding homesteads, annuities and life insurance.
- Avoid mixing business assets with personal assets. That way, if your company runs into a problem, your personal assets may be shielded from risks.

Buying in a Self-Managed SUPER Fund

What Can A Self-Managed Super Do?

- It can invest in shares all over the world.
- It can invest all over the world in managed Funds.
- It can invest all over the world in Options.
- It can invest in any Real Estate, <u>just not your own personal home.</u>
- It can invest in Property Trusts.
- It can invest in valuable collections, such as stamps or coins, and art.
- It can invest in loans belonging to others, except members or their families.

What Can a Self-Managed Super NOT Do?

- It cannot invest in the property you own.
- It cannot lend money to you.
- It cannot borrow money without certain conditions being met. Further explanations on this change are below.
- It cannot purchase assets owned by you or your family or anybody you are associated with.
- It cannot invest in Futures.
- It cannot pay you to manage the fund or investments made.

The following three conditions must be met if the SMSF trustees are going to borrow money to invest:

1. The asset being purchased with borrowed money must be held in the trust until it has been paid in full. When the first payment is made, the trustees of the fund may receive the beneficial interest and a right (not an obligation) to receive legal ownership of the asset held in trust with the payment of all of the installments on the borrowed money.

2. If the borrowed money is defaulted on, the lender's option to default is limited to the asset which was purchased with the borrowed money only. In other words, the lender cannot make a claim against any other asset of the fund, even if the value of the asset does not meet the amount owed on the loan.

3. The amount borrowed cannot be used to purchase an asset that is owned by a fund member. All restrictions to what the SMSF is allowed to purchase are still in effect.

While SMSFs have always been to purchase options, which are always a risky investment, the introduction of the Endowment and Installment Warrants have allowed the SMSFs to also purchase leveraged investments. While more aggressive investors have always had the ability to gain leverage with the SMSF, the changes have allowed greater flexibility in this area.

Advantages & Disadvantages of the Self-Managed Fund

Like everything else in life, there are advantages as well as disadvantages to the self-managed fund which we will discuss below.

Main advantages:

1. The fund pays 15% tax on taxable income of the fund and tax payable is reduced by imputation credits on dividends received by the fund. Capital gains tax on assets held in a self-managed superannuation fund for over twelve months and later sold is equivalent to a flat 10%

2. Trustees (who, as mentioned earlier, are also the members) control investment decisions and asset mix. Trustees also have the flexibility to change investments when they decide appropriate.

3. Individuals avoid yearly fees of about 2%.

4. Self-managed funds encourage self-sufficiency at retirement and interest in one's own financial affairs.

5. The fund can be used to accrue superannuation assets and can then be used to pay a superannuation-funded pension to the members when they retire. This option offers an increased level of financial security later in life.

6. The self-managed fund's costs of compliance and administration are most times less than the fees that are charged by a public superannuation fund. However,

this will vary with the size of the investment, the cost of advice, number of transactions and amounts and types of investments held.

7. The members of the fund do not have to pay an entry fee (of about 6% on every contribution) when they contribute to the fund or an exit fee if they withdraw their benefits.

8. Individuals running a business have the option to own their business premises in a self-managed superannuation fund and rent to themselves or a related party. The self-managed fund also allows individuals to own residential investment property as long as the fund buys it from or leases it to an unrelated party.

9. Self-managed funds can be extremely lucrative and rewarding as soon as you know what you're doing and get the hang of things. One example: self-managed superannuation funds can be selected and, where appropriate, integrated with the members' personal investments in order to get an overall diversification.

10. Well-arranged and managed self-managed superannuation funds look after your assents in the event your superannuation outlives you so that your family and other members benefit.

11. Individuals who make the time to properly understand and follow the rules (and restrictions) will rarely if ever encounter problems with this fund.

With the SMSF, you are in full control of your fund.

The self-managed superannuation fund provides individuals with the opportunity to be involved in their fund's operation and management. Individuals have full control over their investments, including important decisions and even daily activities of the fund. Furthermore, individuals will have flexibility to change their fund's investment strategy should they be required to for any reason including personal circumstances or changing economic conditions.

With the SMSF, you have alternative options.

In the self-managed superannuation fund, individuals have a wider range of investments available to them to tap into. Individuals can attain any asset they feel are appropriate for the investment objectives of their fund, including property, art, bonds or shares investments.

With the SMSF, you collect tax allowances.

The self-managed superannuation fund plays a major role in providing individuals with their retirement funding since they are taxed at a concessional rate, giving their investments a chance to expand at a quicker rate.

With the SMSF, you can claim expense deductions.

Some of the expense deductions you can claim include: office running costs (office equipment, computer, stationary, software, etc.), establishment costs, and many more.

Main disadvantages:

1. Individuals will need to pay ongoing attention to investment, the economy and any modifications in legislation.

2. Probable higher costs of SMSF funds with low capital may make the fund uneconomic should it be compared to the net return from an account in a larger self-managed fund.

3. Since the members are also the trustees, they have additional responsibilities and further requirements to conform to legal requirements.

4. The fund may actually have a lower investment performance should the trustees' (and members') management not be closely controlled or should there be too much dependence on commercial advisers.

5. Should the self-managed fund become non-complying, it may lose its tax concessions.

Individuals are required to give a lot of attention to investment management, and the administrative and tax factors of a self-managed superannuation fund, not only to obtain a lucrative investment management but to also meet all administration and legal obligations that the fund has on trustees.

Your Role and Responsibilities

It is your responsibility to ensure that your fund is complying with all super and tax laws and regulations, even if you do choose to use a super professional such as a financial adviser. It's imperative you fully understand what's involved and get familiar with your responsibilities.

A trustee's duties and responsibilities include:

- Ensuring that the fund's sole purpose is to pay retirement benefits to all members of the fund;
- Accepting contributions and paying benefits;
- Making investment decisions and complying with limitations;
- Ensuring an approved auditor is appointed for every income year;
- Completing administrative tasks (e.g. lodging annual returns, record keeping, etc.);
- Reviewing and updating the fund's trust deed and investment strategy.

Should there be a change in trustees, directors, members, contact details or address, you need to tell the ABR within 28 days via their online service at www.abr.gov.au (can only use this service if you have a primary digital certificate) or lodge a Change of Details for Superannuation Entities fund at:

http://www.ato.gov.au/content/downloads/nat3036.pdf

Investing Your Fund's Money

Unlike other super funds, SMSFs give you more flexibility when it comes to investing your fund's money; you can choose the investment for your fund as long as you follow the super regulations and invest according to:

- Your fund's trust deed;
- Your investment strategy;
- The super laws.

The super fund has not set up rules, telling you what you can and cannot invest in, but they do have various restrictions which your fund is expected to comply with.

For example, trustees cannot:

- Lend the fund's money or offer any kind of financial aid to members/relatives;
- Acquire assets from related parties of the fund, including fund members and all fund employer-sponsors;
- Borrow money on the fund's behalf;
- Lend to/invest in/lease to related parties of the fund more than 5% of the fund's total assets;
- Enter into investments on the fund's behalf that are not made or maintained on an arm's length basis.

Investment Strategies

Investing through a self-managed superannuation fund is just like any other investment you make except with the SMSF, you can't spend the money on anything other than investments until you retire.

You need to approach your SMSF with a long-term attitude towards your investments such as property and equity based investments.

In addition, SMSFs may invest in a unit trust or a company, without that investment being considered an in-house asset, if certain conditions are met. The main conditions being that the trust or company:

- Does not borrow;
- Has no assets with a charge over them;
- Does not loan money to individuals or other entities (other than deposits with authorized deposit-taking institutions);
- Does not acquire an asset from a related party of the superannuation fund other than business real property acquired at market value;
- Does not directly or indirectly lease assets to related parties, other than business real property;
- Does not conduct a business; and
- Conducts all transactions on an arm's length basis.

SMSF & Funding Property Development

The main aspect about whether self-managed funds can use an *installment warrant arrangement* in order to expand real property is that the law demands the borrowed money to be used to attain an asset. Still, there does seem to be a way it can be accomplished.

Let's first look at a solution that may work in your situation.

> **Funding through a partnership arrangement**
- SMSFs can co-expand real property in partnership with a third party external funder.

- The SMSF would attain the undeveloped land under an installment warrant arrangement;
- Third party is expected to contribute 100% of the development, or at least most of it; to finance the partnership. This contribution will generally be unsecured, but if it is directly secured, the security can't involve taking security over the self-managed fund's assets.

➢ **Third party's loan – secured**

In order for a third party's loan to be secured, the third party funder is required to fund both the purchase and development through an Installment Warrant arrangement. As part of the loan to purchasing the site, the third party external funder may:

- Obtain limited-recourse security over the site; and
- Be granted full rights over whatever is constructed on the site.

By doing this, the loan is secured by the lender having rights over what is to be built on the site.

The Australian law allows SMSFs to use Installment Warrant arrangements to attain assets. Constructing an asset through development is not attaining an asset, but creating an asset.

The ATO specifically addressed the issue of attaining an asset is summarized below:

1. Is there an argument that development equates to 'attaining' an asset?

An SMSF may argue that developing a property through construction still means the SMSF attains the building, it is just that it does so over time. However, this presents two primary difficulties:

- First, an external lender is unlikely to be prepared to lend on this basis (at least in the absence of further security — which could not include any other assets of the SMSF). That is, an external lender is unlikely to provide a capital loan which will be used both for acquiring and developing land, which is secured (at least in the beginning) only by an undeveloped parcel of land; and
- Second, because immediately after the acquisition the only asset is undeveloped land, most of the borrowing actually relates to service fees such as construction costs. The new rules require the borrowing to be applied to purchase an 'asset' but these services are not 'assets' and are arguably separate from the tangible asset that will be brought into existence through the construction process.

2. Can an SMSF self-fund a development and then refinance?

If an SMSF has the capital to self-fund construction of a development on undeveloped land, then we need to consider whether, after the completion of the development, it can refinance its new asset through an installment warrant arrangement.

The problem with this strategy, however, is that the SMSF would already own the asset that would form the basis of the installment warrant arrangement. Therefore, money borrowed under the installment warrant arrangement would not be used to attain a new asset.

Under an installment warrant, an SMSF:

- Makes a preliminary payment of a portion of the purchase price of an asset, this can be 25%, for example;
- Unpaid balance of purchase price is efficiently loaned to an SMSF or any other superannuation fund by the issuer of the installment warrant;
- The loan and interest is increasingly paid back by the SMSF through installments until the asset is paid for entirely.

An SMSF is given an interest in the underlying asset and is permitted to all income from the asset for the entire duration of the loan. The lender, who is also the issuer of the installment warrant, is permitted to interest on the loan and is protected. Should the SMSF fail to pay on the borrowing, the lender may have to resort to the original asset only. In other words, the lender will not have another alternative to any other assets.

Since an SMSF is only required to fund the preliminary payment, installment warrants:

Allow an SMSF to use its capital to attain several assets as opposed to committing all or most of its capital towards purchasing a single asset.

Are effective means of SMSFs, influencing the purchase of an asset.

➢ Assets attained through an 'installment warrant' arrangement

Generally speaking, all SMSF assets that allow direct investments (property, shares…) can be attained through an installment warrant arrangement as long as it meets all superannuation law requirements and is permitted by the SMSF's governing rules.

➢ Lender / issuer of the warrant

There are no restrictions regarding who may lend and issue the warrant – in fact, the lender can even be the SMSF's members.

➢ What are the restrictions?

Installment warrant arrangements must take a specific form in order to comply with the new rules:

- The money borrowed has to be used to attain an asset in which the SMSF is not otherwise prohibited from acquiring;
- The asset obtained is required to be held on trust so that the SMSF received beneficial interest in the asset;

- The SMSF has to have the right to obtain legal ownership of the asset by making one or more payments after obtaining the beneficial interest;
- All recourse that the lender has against the SMSF has to be limited to rights regarding the asset obtained.

Should the SMSF fail to pay on the borrowing, the lender will have limited rights in recovering money to repossessing and disposing of the obtained asset and cannot recover money through recourse to the fund's other assets.

Furthermore, an SMSF is required to comply with other legislative requirements (including sole purpose test, investment restrictions relating to in-house assets and assets acquired from related parties). Should the requirements not be met, borrowing money through an installment warrant arrangement will be considered a direct breach of the super laws and will further have civil or criminal consequences for a fund trustee.

> **Installment warrants & real property**

If the SMSF acquires real property from a related party, then:

- The real property must be commercial property acquired at market value; or
- The asset, when attained by the SMSF, must not breach the in-house asset rules.
- Stamp duty will be payable when the SMSF acquires the real property.

- The lender (who effectively issues the warrant) could either be the existing owner of the property, a third party financial institution or a related party of the SMSF.
- Should the SMSF obtain a loan from a related party of the SMSF, the interest rate needs to reflect commercial rates.
- If the real property is a development site, then the purchase price of the site may be funded through an installment warrant arrangement.

SMSF & Buying Residential Property

The Ideal Clients

1. Over 10 years to retirement
2. Stable employment and contributions
3. At least 40% of property purchase price available in a superfund

The Basics

Why borrow in your super fund to buy property?

- It can deliver significantly better after-tax returns compared to traditional borrowing outside super.
- It is an opportunity to diversify a super portfolio and therefore reduce the overall volatility and risk on the portfolio.
- The potential to utilize traditional negative gearing strategies to generate tax-effective income.

- It allows clients to defer any capital gains until retirement, at which stage they become tax free (subject to legislation).
- Asset protection from commercial and Bankruptcy Acts subject of course to anti avoidance rules.

What you Can do	What you CANNOT do
Purchase business property through your SMSF which you can hold as an investment or occupy as an owner occupied business premises	Have owner occupied residential property in your super fund.
Sell/Transfer commercial property already owned to the super fund and release cash that you would otherwise not have been able to access.	Transfer residential property already owned by a related party into your SMSF.
Purchase residential property from an arm's length vendor.	Redraw loan facilities in your super fund.
Purchase the property you would like to retire to, lease it out now and sell it to yourself when you retire and retire richer.	

The ability to transfer commercial property which the members of related entities already own, allows you to unlock cash to:

- Repay non-deductible debt
- Invest in your business
- Invest in other assets
- Re-contribute to your SMSF (subject to individual contributions limits)

Are SMSF loans any different to my home or other investment loans?

Yes – SMSF loans are different. This is because they are linked to superannuation legislation which normal loans are not subject to. There are also important tax implications if certain structures and processes are not adhered to.

Superannuation legislation dictates certain characteristics that these loans must have and therefore the documentation for them is very different to normal loans.

This is why it is important to have experts in this field helping you find the right solutions for your particular situation. That's where advice is important.

How it Works

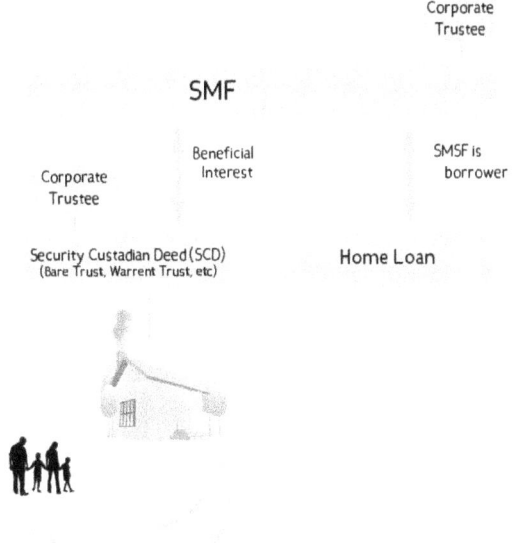

This is a complex transaction that we are going to make very simple.

1. You need a Self-Managed Super Fund (SMSF) to undertake this transaction. The trustee of the SMSF is the borrower.

2. The property must be held in a trust which is called a Security Custodian Trust (SCD). This trust may also be referred to as the purchasing trust, special trust or bare trust. All of these terms just mean that this is the vehicle which holds the property on trust for your SMSF.

3. The trustee of the SCD is the entity which is the purchaser on the sale contract that you enter into. The trustee of this trust must be different to the trustee of your SMSF.

4. The beneficiary of the SCD is your SMSF.

5. The Mortgage is given to the lender by the trustee of the SCD to secure your SMSF loan.

By Mark Robinson and Lars Huttner

Price vs. Cost

		Own home	Normal investment property	SMSF investment property
Tax rate		46.50%	46.50%	15%
Purchase price		500,000	500,000	500,000
Deposit	28%	140,000	140,000	140,000
Total cost of deposit		261,682	261,682	164,706
Loan		360,000	360,000	360,000
30 year P&I (pm)	5.70%	2,089	2,089	2,089
Total repayments		752,199	752,199	752,199
Total interest		392,199	392,199	392,199
Total COST of				
Principal		672,897	672,897	423,529
Interest		733,082	392,199	392,199
Total Cost of Loan		1,405,979	1,065,096	815,728
Total COST of Deposit		261,682	261,682	164,706
Total COST of property		1,667,662	1,326,778	980,434
				346,344 Less
SMSF Savings		687,227	346,344	
		41%	26%	
Purchase Price		500,000	500,000	500,000
Value after 30 years	6%	2,871,746	2,871,746	2,871,746
Capital Gains Tax		0	551,431	0
Total outlay		1,667,662	1,326,778	980,434
Total return		2,871,746	2,320,315	2,871,746
Profit		**1,204,084**	**993,536**	**1,891,311**
				897,775 More

How to Make Money from Property During a Recession

Many property investors worry about recessions and try to sell before a recession hits, often missing the greatest capital appreciation in the property market. Having strong growth for many years does not mean that the property bubble is going to burst as you often hear in the media. This is often mentioned after a period of strong growth, but often strong growth is followed by even stronger growth before a slowdown. Our strategy is to hold the property, through boom times and through recessions, to achieve the long-term compounding effect of high growth.

If you sell your growth property with the plan to buy lower and go back in later, your outlay in selling costs, capital gains tax and repurchase costs will almost always ensure you don't come out in a better position at the end. And that's only if you manage to pick the top and bottom, which you can never do except with hindsight.

Now, let's have a look at how we can benefit from recessions.

During, recessions, many people lose their jobs, many businesses struggle, banks and lenders become more edgy and do not tolerate missed payments, and they repossess more properties and restrict lending overall. All this has the effect of reducing the number of buyers and increasing the number of properties on the market. Many property owners, facing repossessions or not being able to afford their mortgage, become desperate to sell especially as the number of buyers reduces significantly. If you are able to buy during recession times, you will certainly get some amazing bargains. Enquire about how long the property has been on the market, assess the market price based on your comparable property analysis, check it out thoroughly and make a low offer. In recessionary times, you can afford to make a lower offer and wait. Just remember to make sure you make an offer on the right property, not just a bargain on the wrong property.

So, do not be worried about recessions. Quite the opposite, you should keep money on the side and try to benefit from recessions. If you're not well prepared and you have borrowed to the hilt, then there is nothing you can do to benefit when a recession hits. So be well prepared and treat recessions as great opportunities to buy properties at bargain prices.

Here's a basic guideline:

- **Buy and Hold** – Buy growth properties at bargain prices ready for the up-swing. It's unlikely you would get these properties at the recession prices again.
- **Add Value** – Create your own growth, not relying on when the market will kick-start again.
- **Future Rezoning** – Properties that are at some stage in the rezoning process are due to increase in value once the rezoning takes effect. In a recession, often the premium that had begun to accumulate because of the future rezoning is all but lost and you can pick some of these up at normal single site prices.

Appendix A: Glossary

Capital Growth

An increase in value from investments that exceeds the purchase price, resulting in increased equity. This can be either natural (market growth) or manufactured (added value growth).

Chattels

Any item/s in the property that may not be a part of the basic structure, such as microwave ovens or other moveable assets are classed as chattels. It is important to recognise that you need to consult a quantity surveyor who will be able to identify all the chattels in the property as they could be depreciated against the property. (See Deprecation for more information)

Closing Costs

All costs associated with purchasing a property. These include the stamp duty on the property, loan fees, legal fees, mortgage insurance (if applicable) and any other associated costs that may be involved in the acquisition.

Compound Interest

Compound Interest is the interest that is calculated on both the principal and the accrued interest. This is a very powerful law and it applies both rate and time. Eventually, it will reach a point called critical mass and this is where the growth is exponential.

Cross-Securitization

Cross-securitisation is defined as a loan that is reliant upon more than one property for security. (I.e. Two or more properties securing one loan) This means that if something went wrong with one property then all other properties "attached" or crossed with that property will go down with it, just like dominos. This is not a good structure to build a portfolio with, and you will find that most banks will try and cross-securitise you every time. This gives the lender greater power; for example, if you decide to sell your investment property, your lender could insist that you use the profits from the sale to pay down your existing home loan. It also complicates your ability to efficiently refinance down the track. To put it simply, the banks will try and make it hard for you to shop elsewhere so of course they will want to structure it that way.

Debt-to-Service Ratio (DSR)

DSR or "Debt Serviceability Ratio" is a percentage of income to debt. This is an important tool to all lenders as they use it to assess your capacity to repay. DSR is usually referred as the cash flow (or serviceability) part of the equation – as opposed to LVR which remember, is the equity (or security) part of the equation. Generally speaking, DSR is a snapshot of your income vs. your expenses to determine if you are capable of repaying a loan. Having too much of one and not enough of the other does constitute a problem and therefore needs to be adjusted. The ideal situation is a good mix of the two. When you're setting up your portfolio, the main focus should be to get LVR and DSR in balance.

Here is a useful link to get an indication of what you may be able to borrow from a serviceability perspective only (security, or deposit is not taken into consideration). Remember this is only an indication and its best to seek professional assistance as different banks have different sensitised rates, which means you will have a varying amount of loan amounts that you could get. Link:

http://www.realestate.com.au/cgi-bin/rsearch?a=calc&cu=fn-rea&jar=BorrowingPower

Depreciation

Depending on the age of the property, you can claim the depreciating values of the fixtures and fittings as well as the raw construction costs of the building. Essentially, the newer the property, the higher the amount of depreciation you can claim against your taxable income, which means more money in your pocket come tax time. These are also known as "on-paper losses" as it is not a physical loss out of your pocket that you are paying for, rather the loss is generated from the depreciating values of the building and/or items which makes it a loss on paper only.

Equity

Equity is the difference between the market value of a property and the outstanding loan amount against it. For example if you owned a property worth $250,000 and you have a loan outstanding on the property for $150,000, then you have $100,000 in equity. A proportion of the equity (depending on the LVR ratio) can be used for a number of different things including deposits for additional properties, cash for lifestyle, boat, shoes, diamonds and so on and so forth. An important thing to note here is to never mix tax effective and non-tax effective funds, it creates a nightmare for the accountant and you go potentially forgo future tax deductions.

So how do we calculate how much equity we can use from our existing properties…?

Calculating your available equity is quite simple; you just subtract what is currently owed on your property from its overall value. For example, let's say you owe the banks $250,000 and your home valuation came in at $500,000 (currently 50% LVR). And let's assume that you wish to only go up to an LVR of 80%, then borrowing up to 80% of $500,000 gives you an amount of $400,000.

If you subtract the balance outstanding of $250,000 from $400,000, you have $150,000 in available equity at 80% LVR which could be used for a deposit and/or costs on other investment properties. You can borrow more than 80% LVR; however this will incur additional fees due to having to pay mortgage insurance.

Exclusive Agency

This is where the owner of a property appoints only one real estate agent to be the exclusive agent in that property's sale. This means that the exclusive agent will get paid a commission for the sale of the property no matter who sells it, including if the owners sell it, whilst under the exclusive agency agreement. The exclusive agency period is usually over a period of 8 weeks. After this point the property or "listing" becomes available to other agents to sell the property.

Holding Costs

The total costs involved in owning a property. This includes all interest on borrowed funds (including capital invested, if applicable), rates, insurances, body corporate fees (if applicable), maintenance, taxes, property management fees, and so on and so forth. Basically every cost associated with owning and maintaining a property.

Internal Rate of Return

This is the most accurate measure of the performance of an investment property. The yield (most commonly used measurement) is just a snap shot of the performance of the property, whereas I.R.R takes into consideration time. The yield is more commonly used by investors; this is mainly due to the ease of calculation and gives you an indication of the performance only. The I.R.R is more difficult to calculate which is why I use a software program called Property Investment Analysis (P.I.A) which calculates this for me within a matter of minutes.

The Internal Rate of Return (IRR) is a measure of the return on a series of cash flows where the time factor is taken into account. To understand the Internal Rate of Return, think of the money you are outlaying on your investment property as being deposited in a bank account, with the interest added each year. In this case the "Deposits" are represented as the after-tax cash flows.

The total amount in your "account" (including interest) at the end of the period is the equity in the investment property. The IRR represents the effective "interest rate" that you have received, but with one important difference: because the interest remains in the property, it is not taxed. The internal rate of return is also calculated and presented for the case where the property is sold and where selling costs and capital gains tax are taken into account.

Landlord's Insurance

Landlords Insurance is a policy of insurance that will protect a property owner from losses that may occur from the property. This is important to check went sourcing a policy as there is different ones available. It may be beneficial to use an insurance broker so they can shop around for the correct policy to suit your needs. Some important things to ensure are covered by your policy are: Loss of rent due to malicious damage, loss of rent due tenant leaving without notice, fire and theft, and contents insurance.

Lenders Mortgage Insurance (LMI)

LMI is a policy of insurance that protects a lender from losses due to default on the loan. Most lenders currently only charge LMI when you go over an 80% LVR. This does not mean to never go over 80% LVR; it just means that it costs you more to borrow the money. In many case in the early stages of my investing, I was well above the 80% mark and I got charged LMI, however the profits and growth and far out weight the extra small cost to borrow the money. There is no fixed way to calculate LMI as it depends on the loan amount that one is applying for and how much over the 80% LVR it is.

Line of Credit (LOC)

A line of credit, generally speaking, is like a big credit card, except it is an Interest only facility where you do not have to repay the principal during the life of the loan. You can only set up this facility using available existing equity that you already have in another asset which will act as security for the LOC. If you take out a line of credit, you can draw on any available funds up to your maximum limit at any time. You can then repay, borrow again whenever you want, up to the limit without needing to re-apply for credit. I also call these internal loans, as all the transactions occur within the loan itself and not a separate account, unlike the offset facilities. It's very important if you are using LOC to not mix tax effective and non-tax effective expenses as causes many issues at the end of the financial year when the account is trying to work out what was used for investment purposes and what was used for living purposes. Always keep these separate!

Loans: Fixes Interest Loans

Fixed Interest loans are when the interest rate at the time of "locking it in" remains static and does not fluctuate during the time period in which you selected at the time. This can be over 1 year, 2 years or 5 years depending on what you want to do at the time. Fixing loans is only used as a cash flow management tool, so you can make your repayments (predictable) if this is what you choose.

Loans: Interest-Only Loans

This is a loan that requires no repayment of the principle, but rather only repayment of the interest accrued on the amount loaned. This is mainly used when you want to maximise your cash flow for further use, either for lifestyle or additional investments.

Loans: Principal and Interest Loans

This is a loan that requires both a repayment of the principle and the interest accrued on the loan. In this case, you are slowly reducing the "amount" of the loan as you are paying a portion of the principal each time you make a repayment. This loan type is best used for your non-tax effective debts i.e. Your Primary Place of Residence (family home) as you are reducing the amount of non-tax effective debt.

Loans: Variable Loans

A loan that has an interest rate that is subject to fluctuation due to economic market conditions. The Reserve Bank of Australia (RBA) gets together on the first Tuesday of every month to decide what action they will take on the interest rate (cash rate), then it is officially announced to the public on the following day. Please take note that the RBA set the cash interest rate, not the banks interest rate. It's the banks that set the interest rate and the individual institutions adjust their rates as they see fit. For example, if the RBA drop rates by 25 basis points (or 0.25%) the banks may not pass that down to the end user. (You and I)

Loan-to-Value Ratio (LVR)

LVR or "Loan to Value Ratio" is the percentage of the amount lent against the value of the property. LVR is usually referred to as the equity part of the equation. When assessing your available equity, we will always base ourselves on a conservative asset value using 80% LVR. Generally financial institutions will lend 80% of the value of the asset.

The reason for that is that on an 80% LVR there will be no Lender's Mortgage Insurance (LMI). The value of the property is determined by an official valuation conducted by a professional entity found on the lender's list of approved Valuers. You will often find that the market value of your property will not match the official valuation because banks will generally take a risk free approach when it comes to lending. It is known that banks will take an additional safety net when it comes to valuations and that in the event of default by the borrower, the bank will want to sell the property as quickly as possible and therefore they mostly sell it below the market value.

LVR Example

Loan to Value Ratio (LVR)

Value $300K →

= LVR 95%

Negatively Geared Property

Negative gearing is a form of financial leverage where an investor borrows money to buy a property, but the income generated by that property does not cover the interest on the loan. It is possible to have a negatively geared, cash flow positive property and this can only be achieved from certain properties with high depreciation (see deprecation for details). If the depreciation is high enough, you can receive a tax refund that if totalled with the rental income it becomes higher than the overall interest repayments; the property is cash flow positive in your hand but making a loss on paper.

Offset Accounts

An offset account is a separate savings account where the balance is offset daily against the loan amount for interest calculation purposes. For example, if you have a loan with $200,000 owing and an offset account with a credit balance of $20,000, in effect, you will only pay interest on $180,000.

These facilities I call external loans as the transactions occur "outside" of the loan, therefore it is much cleaner for the accountant because the loan itself is not changing only the offset account. So if you mix up tax effective expenses and non-tax effective expenses in the offset account it doesn't cause an issue with the accountant and/or tax refunds.

Open-Listed

This is a listing agreement in where multiple real estate agents may be employed to sell the property. The owner pays a commission only to the agent who finds the buyer. This listing is also known as a simple listing or a general listing and the owner is not obligated to pay anyone a commission if the owner personally sells the property. Such a listing is often used by builders and developers who agree to pay a sales commission to any agent who sells a house or lot in their subdivision. This method of selling can be a great disadvantage to the seller because it will reduce the chance of achieving the highest sale price, and the agents will almost certainly make little or no effort to sell the property for that person knowing that other agents can sell it as well.

Positive Cash-Flow

When revenues can cover operating costs.

Positively Geared Property

Positive gearing occurs when you borrow to invest in an income producing property and the returns (income) from that property exceed all of the associated costs of borrowing. These properties are usually found in more rural areas, where capital growth will not be very significant over the short term. There are ways that you can create positive cash flow properties in areas where growth is very solid.

Return on Investment (ROI) – 1st

Not a lot of people are aware of this in the industry and almost everyone refers to ROI as Return ON Investment. This is true; however, the reason I have put this here for you to understand and put (1st), is because this is the first thing you want to get a return back on. For example if you put $50,000 into a property deal, will you get the $50,000 back straight away…? The deals you want to be doing are the deals where you will initially get your invested capital back, and then the Return ON investment comes 2nd. (See below for Return On Investment Definition)

Return On Investment (ROI) – 2nd

This is the financial benefits flowing from an investment, typically expressed as an annual percentage of the amount invested. Therefore, it is simply the percentage of return that you receive from your investment against your deposit (Capital Invested). Example shown in below table:

Return ON Investment Example - Assume that you purchased a Property for $150,000 at Fair Market Value with an 80% Lend	
Deposit + Closing costs (assume $6000)	$ 36,000.00
Borrow	$ 120,000.00
Interest Paid (Assume 9% interest rate)	$ 10,800.00
Income (Rent $150/wk including 2% vacancy rate)	$ 7,644.00
Expenses (Rates, Insurance etc) Assume $2500	$ 2,500.00
Net Income	$ 5,144.00
PRE-TAX Negative Cash flow	-$ 5,656.00
Tax Rebate (31.5%) (assume no other deductions)	$ 1,782.00
Cash Contribution Needed	$ 3,874.00
Capital Growth (Assume 8%)	$ 12,000.00
Net Total Return	$ 8,126.00
After Tax Return on Investment (Capital Invested)	8126/36000
ROI (%)	22.57%

Sole Agency

Sole agency is similar to exclusive agency, where there is only one agent with the rights to sell the property, however, the owner can sell the property themselves and if they manage to do this then the agent does not get paid any commission.

Please note: If you can find out whether an agent has an open listing, sole agency or exclusive agency (without asking them!) it can make it interesting when buying and can create great opportunities for negotiations.

Stand-Alone Equity Release

The process of unlocking some of the value held in a property and turning that useable cash. This is the way in which you want to structure your long term portfolio. It gives you the power, not the banks, due to you having the flexibility to use other banks easily without expensive fees and transaction issues.

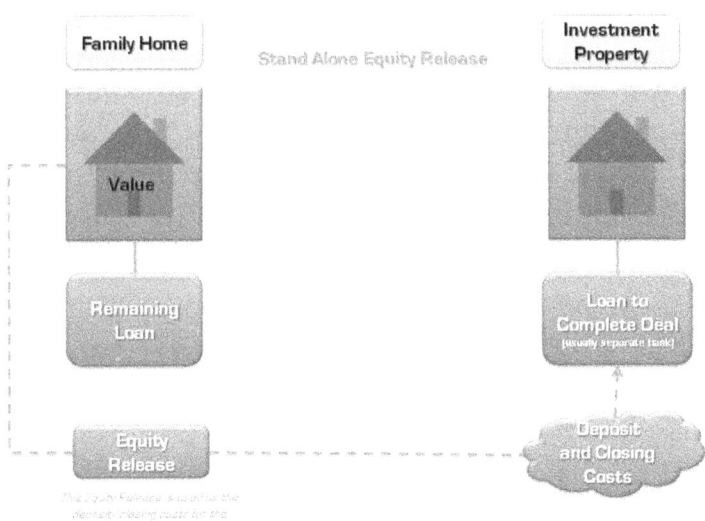

Even using this structure within the same bank is still effective as you can control where your money goes and not them. Most lenders will try and cross-collateralise (cross-securitise) you as they limit your options then as it becomes a costly exercise to go to another lender.

Stamp Duty (for Property)

There are many different types of stamp duties. The most common one when investing in property is the transfer duties where the ownership of the property is transferred from one party to another. (It's just like a form of tax that the government charges). There are other stamp duties involved in the purchasing of a property which is on the loan. The main thing to understand here is that the stamp duty on an investment property is much higher than that of an owner occupied property, and that stamp duty is calculated differently from state to state. To give you an idea of how much stamp duty cost, please click on the link below and play around with the figures and different states, you will then see how much this costs.

Link: http://www.realestate.com.au/cgi-bin/rsearch?a=calc&cu=fn-rea&jar=StampDuty

Note: Always remember to add this cost into your figures when analysing deals. These costs form part of your closing costs.

Tax Deductible

This is generally any expense related to your investment property that you can claim against your taxable income.

These can be variable amounts that you can subtract, or deduct, from your gross income. As a result, the tax deduction will lower overall taxable income and thus lower the amount of tax paid. The exact amount of tax savings is dependent on your individual rate of tax. I always make sure when I'm working with an accountant, that they have got personal experience in property investment themselves as they will know all the items you can claim – Extremely important.

Vendor

This is when someone is referring to the current owner of the property, typically the seller of the property.

Vendor Finance

Vendor financing can be a very lucrative strategy if a buyer wants to start investing and doesn't have a deposit. It is where the buyer negotiates with the vendor (owner) to supply them with an amount of money, typically the deposit amount, where the buyer agrees to pay them back after a certain period of time. Basically the vendor acts as a bank to the buyer and the terms and conditions are decided between them.

Yield

Yield is your yearly return on investment that is usually expressed as a percentage. There are a number of yields that can be used in property to compare investments—the most common of which is rental yield, which is the annual rental income divided by the purchase price as a percentage.

What's the rental yield for a property that is rented for $250/week and the purchase price is $300,000. The answer is 4.33%.

Note: The yield is only a snap shot of the performance of the property and should only be used for a quick guide. The real returns are calculated by the Internal Rate of Return (IRR).

Appendix B: Property Checklists

Simple Reno. Checklist

Kitchen
Cupboards
Bench Tops
Handles
Sink
Tiling
Taps/mixer
Rangehood
Gas cooktop
Oven

Bathroom
Tiling
Mirror
Vanity
Shower Screen
Bath
Bath Resurface
Taps/shower head
Plumbing
Extractor fan

Laundry
Trough
Tiling
Vinyl
Taps/shower head
Plumbing

General Interior
Floor Sanding/Polishing
Carpets
Vinyl
Paint inside
Curtains/Blinds

Built in Robes
Air Con
Electrical
Light Fittings
Light switches/power points
Doors
Door furniture (handles)
Cleaning
Plumbing
Electrical
Skip Bin Hire
General materials
Leaks/damp/mould

Outside
Render
Landscaping
Retic
Paving
Roof Repair
Paint outside
Patio
Washing line
Post box
Fence
Clearing

Property Condition Checklist

With experience, you will be able to assess the sate of a property from the first look and see the renovation work that it needs and the cost involved. You should fill in the inspection checklist below. Initially, and until you have done several of these renovations, under no circumstances, should you buy a property for renovation until you have fully assessed the costs involved and obtained several quotations. Get your builder and contractors in and get some quotes, fully assess the situation, and understand what you're getting yourself into.

When you inspect a property that needs renovation, you need to watch out for the following costly items. Keep in mind that these are serious renovations that don't necessarily add value but that DO add a great deal of cost to your project.

These types of renovations are not recommended as they are not the sort of refurbishments that will build the property's equity. However, these particular concerns are common in the types of homes that may need general refurbishment.

Object	Things to look for	Checklist
Roof	The roof is usually a major expense and you have to carefully inspect it to ensure there is no major work required to the roof. A few missing slates or tiles, is not a problem, but check if they have left any damage. If too many are missing, check the type of construction, e.g. are they fixed by nailing them to the roof and if so are most of the nails rusty and breaking off. If so, you may need to take the whole roof out and re-lay it which would be pretty expensive. Also check the roof line, is it sagging badly, go inside the roof, check the construction, if it's timber, are there any sign of rot or infestation. Do roof trusses need replacing?	
Dampness and moulds	Are there any obvious issues with dampness and moulds? Look in the basement, in the dark smelly areas, behind cupboards, under the stairs, at the walls, behind cabinets and especially at bottom of the wall and behind skirting boards (on the ground floor and basement only). Is there dampness in any area of the house? Treating rising dampness itself is not very expensive but the overall job can be if it has spread throughout the house, as in addition to treating the affected areas, you have to take out all the wall lining or plastering, treat the dampness and moulds, then re-plaster and decorate.	

Object	Things to look for	Checklist
Rot and infestation	Wood condition: Are there any obvious issues with rot throughout the house? Are there any small holes in any of the property's woodwork that may be signs of woodworm infestation or rot? If so has the problem been treated? Inspect all the woodwork, check it out for any infestation, look under the carpets in wooden floor houses, in the corners, inside built in cupboards, in the basement, under the stairs. Check the windows, doors as well. Are there any obvious issues with termites or other pests throughout the house? If there is a problem, you really need to assess how far it has spread in the house. If it has spread, it could be quite expensive and may require the replacement of roof trusses, joists, floorboards, and so on.	
Plumbing	Does the property require a full re-plumbing?	
Electric wiring	Does the property require full re-wiring?	
External	Are any major external works required? E.g. rendering all external walls could be expensive especially if it requires scaffolding and you need to hack out the existing layer.	
Other	Look out for any other major items or structural problems.	

Preparing a Property Plan

1st, your goals and preferences will help design your strategy

- Just as a reminder, here is a summary of the main strategies:
- Buy and hold in high growth areas to compound growth and build equity (basic investment strategy)
- Positive cash flow strategy for income (basic investment strategy)
- Profitable add-value-and-sell projects to generate extra income (advanced)
- Other advanced strategies: Refurbishments, subdivisions that retain the home, land subdivisions, developments, buying in advance of zoning changes
- Or a combination of these strategies

1. What is your risk tolerance

    Obviously, like any other business investment higher returns always mean higher risk. So accelerating growth carries higher risk but also higher potential rewards.

    ☐ Low risk tolerance
    ☐ Average tolerance
    ☐ High risk tolerance

Strategies for low risk tolerance:

- ☐ Buy property for a low LVR (loan to value ratio).
- ☐ Check that you could afford the mortgage payments at 5 points higher interest rate
- ☐ Reserve a buffer of 1 year's interest stored in an offset account attached to your mortgage.
- ☐ Choose basic investment strategies until you're 100% confident to move to more advanced strategies

Strategies for average risk tolerance

- ☐ Not more than 80% LVR (loan to value ratio).
- ☐ Check that you could afford the mortgage payments at 3 points higher interest rate
- ☐ Reserve a buffer of 6 months interest stored in an offset account attached to your mortgage.
- ☐ Start with basic investment strategies and if you feel confident move to more advanced strategies and build a portfolio of both

Strategies for high risk tolerance

- ☐ A high LVR (loan to value ratio) is fine but ensure you can handle rate increases and have a cash buffer.
- ☐ Use advanced and combination strategies to accelerate your growth
- ☐ Buy, add-value and sell to generate high cash amounts
- ☐ Reinvest into the high growth buy-and-holds and into future rezoning buy-and-holds

Objectives

2. What is the primary objective of your property investment?

   Choose only one:

   ☐ Regular income ☐ Growth in wealth

   If you chose regular growth in wealth, you can skip the next question.

   Regular income:

   If you are looking for a regular income you need to adopt positive cash flow properties. These properties produce an income but generally show low growth. You are not creating wealth here, you're generating income.

3. Are you looking for:

   ☐ Short term income (immediate)
   ☐ Medium term income (6 months to 2 years)
   ☐ Long term income (5 years plus)

Short term income:

If you're looking for short term income, then:

Strategy #1   Go for positive cash flow properties which will produce a positive cash flow as soon as they are rented out. You'll need either:

   ☐ several positive cash flow properties as each one usually produces only a small amount of surplus income.

☐ A low LVR (loan to value ratio) with a bigger cash injection can give you positive cash flow, but is not necessarily optimising your return on investment or your tax benefits.

Medium term income:

If you're looking for income in the medium term, then:

Strategy #1 Go for positive cash flow properties which will produce a positive cash flow as soon as they are rented out. You'll need either:

☐ several positive cash flow properties as each one usually produces only a small amount of surplus income.

☐ A low LVR (loan to value ratio) with a bigger cash injection can give you positive cash flow, but is not necessarily optimising your return on investment or your tax benefits.

Strategy #2 Buy a property for an add value project (such as a refurbishment with subdivision). Add the value and then either

☐ sell the added value property or properties and use the cash profit as your required extra income

☐ Rent out at an increased rent if this produces positive cash flow, or

☐ Sell half of a subdivided property and put the proceeds into the mortgage while you keep and rent out the other half of the subdivided property. That will improve the cash flow and if it's the right project it can give you a small positive cash flow.

This strategy will require that you have enough cash to do the work needed to add value.

Long term income:

Strategy #1   Buy a property for an add value project (such as a refurbishment with subdivision). Add the value and then either

☐ sell the added value property or properties and use the cash profit as your required extra income

☐ Rent out at an increased rent if this produces positive cash flow, or

☐ Sell half of a subdivided property and put the proceeds into the mortgage while you keep and rent out the other half of the subdivided property. That will improve the cash flow and if it's the right project it can give you a small positive cash flow.

☐ This strategy will require that you have enough cash to do the work needed to add value.

Strategy #2   You can adopt the "buy and hold" strategy in high growth areas which besides producing significant growth, will start producing a surplus income after a few years as rent increases catch up with the mortgage interest which remains more or less the same.

4. Are you looking for?

    ☐ Short term small increase in growth:

    ☐ You need to adopt strategies that add value as this is the only way to get the growth within a short period of time.

    ☐ Medium term large increase in growth:

    ☐ For medium term you can combine strategies such as adding value and then holding on to the property. This will accelerate growth and get you a larger increase in the medium term.

    ☐ Long term considerable increase growth:
    You can adopt Buy and hold strategy in high growth areas (with or without adding value)

5. Which choice most meets your objectives?

    For further details about yield and growth

    ☐ Yield 12%, growth 2%

    ☐ Yield 10%, growth 4%

    ☐ Yield 8%, growth 6%

    ☐ Yield 6%, growth 8%

    ☐ Yield 4%, growth 10%

    ☐ Yield 2%, growth 12%

> ***Important point:*** These figures are very general guidelines. For example, a 12% yield in residential property is very hard to achieve, even with refurbishment, though not impossible. On the growth side, in an area with a proven growth of 10% p.a., you're more likely to get a yield of 3% than 4%. So use these as strategy guidelines, not absolute targets!

- ☐ Yield 12%, growth 2%: You're looking for income here, adopt positive cash flow strategy. Go for the property with the highest yield. Find a property to be renovated to be able to achieve such a high yield and then rent it out.
- ☐ Yield 10%, growth 4%: You're looking for income here, adopt a positive cash flow strategy. Go for the property with the highest yield but bear in mind the growth in the area. Look for renovations if you can find them in your target area.
- ☐ Yield 8%, growth 6%: You're looking for a good income and moderate growth, adopt positive cash flow strategy and thoroughly search for the highest growth area that you can find to produce this yield.
- ☐ Yield 6%, growth 8%: You're looking for moderate income and higher growth; adopt "buy & hold" strategy while increasing income by renovation or subdivision or other add value strategies.
- ☐ Yield 4%, growth 10%: You're looking for low income and high growth; adopt "buy & hold" strategy in high growth areas with or without add value strategies.

☐ Yield 2%, growth 12%: You're looking for the highest possible growth; adopt "buy & hold" strategy in the highest growth area you can find and use add value strategies to accelerate the growth.

Check where you have chosen to be on the growth/yield balance and cross-check with your primary objective to ensure it correlates with your goals.

6. Which property types most meet your objectives?

   For further details about property types, refer to chapter "Types of Property" in this book.

The town or city I am going to invest in is:

_____ and my reasons are:

1. _____
2. _____
3. _____

The suburbs I'm focusing on initially are:

1. _____ Reason: _____
2. _____ Reason: _____
3. _____ Reason: _____

Congratulations! You're ready to do your preliminary property plan.

Finance

I can borrow up to:	$ _____
I have cash available of:	$ _____
The amount I can borrow against my equity is:	$ _____
My initial purchase budget is:	$ _____

Structure

This is my ownership structure:

Structure type _____

Reason I have chosen this structure
_____

Whose name will the property be bought in?
_____

Goals

This is what I want to achieve with property investment:

1. _____
2. _____
3. _____

Property

This is my property brief:

Type of property _____

_____

_____

City _____

Suburbs 1. _____

2. _____

3. _____

Strategy

These are the strategies I will start with:

Strategies or combinations

1. _____
2. _____
3. _____

This is the help I'll need

1. _____
2. _____
3. _____

This what I'll handle by myself

1. _____
2. _____
3. _____

Action plan

The next steps I need to take are:

Action Step or result to achieve	Date by which I'll do it	Completed (Tick and date)
1.		
2.		
3.		
4.		
5.		

Review and update at least once every month

Progress monitor

This is your current net property wealth:

_____

Update the figure every time you buy or sell a property. At least every 12 months estimate the values and monitor how the growth in value of each property is increasing over time. The true measure of your success is in how your total equity is increasing over time.

At your annual review, confirm whether the reasons to hold each property are still valid. Only sell if:

(a) You have to

(b) You have reached your goals and selling is part of the plan

(c) The reasons for holding the properties are no longer valid

Expansion:

- Build your Portfolio by acquiring more property through refinancing using the equity that has built up.
- Adopt more advanced strategies together with strong buy and holds to accelerate your growth as you gain more experience.

Congratulations, *you've just set up your Property Plan!*

Special Offer

Would you like to find out if property is the right vehicle for your situation?

Book in right now for your **FREE** investment property strategy session, your bonus for reading this book.

To Grab Your Bonus Session go to

www.WinningtheWealthGame.com.au/propertybookoffer

In this personalized session you will get a property plan tailored just for you.

We'll discuss what options are available for you and what your next step is.

Other Books in the Series

Winning The Wealth Game by Protecting Your Assets

Winning The Wealth Game In Business

Winning The Wealth Game With Shares

Winning the Wealth Game by Creating Multiple Streams of Income

Winning the Wealth Game Online

Winning the Wealth Game in Network Marketing

www.ingramcontent.com/pod-product-compliance
Lightning Source LLC
Chambersburg PA
CBHW050552160426
43199CB00015B/2634